AF506668

The Poetic Edda

The Legends of the Viking Age

By

Quinton Elsken

Brewer Publishing Searcy, Arkansas 2026

PUBLISHED BY BREWER PUBLISHING

https://www.brewerpublishing.net/

Brewer Publishing is an Anti-GenAI company and a Pro-LGBTQIA+ company

The colophon is a trademark of Brewer Publishing.

Library of Congress Cataloging-in-Publication Data
Elsken, Quinton
The Poetic Edda: poems / by Quinton Elsken. —1st ed.
p. 402 cm. 15.24x22.86
ISBN: 979-8-9945671-1-1
LCCN: 2026935914
https://lccn.loc.gov/2026935914

Copyedited by: Dakota McCoy
Internal Art by: Konley Runyon
Cover by: Nich Bell

Manufactured in the United States of America
First Edition

To my mother and father, my guiding lights,

to Zane, Eden, and Alec, my rocks in the storm,

to JB, Oatmeal, and Raisin, my furry companions,

to China, Simba, and Rocket, forever loved and dearly missed.

Acknowledgements

I owe an immense debt of gratitude to the National and University Library of Iceland, for their operation of the website handrit.is, on which they have uploaded scans of numerous medieval manuscripts, including the *Codex Regius, AM 748 I 4to, Hauksbók, Flateyarbók, Codex Wormianus*, and numerous manuscripts of *Hervarar Saga ok Heiðreks*, all of which were used as sources for this book.

I am similarly thankful to the Árni Magnússon Institute for Icelandic Studies and the Arnamagnæan Institute for allowing scans of the manuscripts in their collections to be uploaded to the internet.

The book would have been impossible without the generosity and transparency of these organizations.

I also owe an unpayable debt to the unknown individuals who first composed these poems, to their many descendants who passed them down the generations, and to the scribes who first committed them to writing. Without their efforts, our knowledge of Norse literature would be irreparably diminished.

Table of Contents

Introduction

Sometime around the year 1220, the Icelandic politician and poet Snorri, son of Sturla, completed a book entitled *Edda*, now known as the *Prose Edda*. It was intended as a textbook of sorts, containing information about the traditional alliterative poetry employed by the Norse people, and stories explaining the origins of many of the poetic terms and kennings (poetic circumlocutions, such as calling a sword a "blood-snake" or a skeleton a "flesh-frame") used in old poetry. In this book, Snorri quotes extensively from poetry that appears to be genuinely pagan in origin, poetry that must once have circulated in oral tradition, but long since disappeared. In the centuries after Snorri's death, *Edda* became a standard text for the study of traditional poetry, and many scholars who studied his book suspected that there had once been a collection of pagan poems that Snorri had drawn from, which in folklore came to be called the *Elder Edda*.

This assumption persisted for centuries, until the year 1643, when the bishop of Skalholt, Iceland, a man named Brynjólfur Sveinsson, acquired a previously unknown medieval document: a collection of thirty pagan poems describing the adventures of the Norse gods, especially Oðin, the all-knowing, one-eyed, many-named god of war and death, and Þor, the devil-slaying god of storms, as well as those of mortal heroes. It seemed that at last the *Elder Edda* had been found. Brynjólfur sent this document to Copenhagen in 1662 as a gift to King Frederick III of Denmark, from which the manuscript has gotten its modern name of *Codex Regius,* Latin for "Royal Book". Later scholarship has shown that the *Regius* was not written down until around the 1270s, many decades after Snorri wrote his *Edda*, and that the two probably drew from the same oral traditions, rather than Snorri having used the *Regius* itself as a source, as was once believed. Nonetheless, it has formed the foundation for all modern versions of the *Elder Edda*, which is now called the *Poetic Edda*.

Over time, other manuscripts have been found that contain even more poems written in the same meters and covering similar subject matter as those in the *Regius*, many of which have found their way into modern editions of the *Poetic Edda*, including this one. These poems constitute one of the primary sources for modern knowledge about the pre-Christian mythology and religious beliefs of the Norse people, and some of them are among the very few surviving examples of Norse pagan literature to have survived the centuries.

There have been many translations of the *Edda* into English over the centuries. The first wave of these, written between the late 18th and early 20th centuries, are quite poetic, but suffer from legibility issues on account of their use of archaic, pseudo-Shakespearian language (*hight, fain, I rede thee*, etc.). In contrast, later translations of the late 20th and early 21st centuries suffer from the opposite issue; they are written in plain, readable modern English, but often lack the poetic effect of the originals and of the older translations due to being written in prose (or "free verse", a kind term for prose with line breaks). My hope for this book is to provide a middle ground between these two options: a poetic translation that is written in language intelligible to a modern reader.

The primary meter chosen for this translation is blank verse (unrhymed iambic pentameter), with some poems in common meter (alternating iambic tetrameter and trimeter) and a few in other meters. This decision was made primarily due to the difficulty of replicating Old Norse poetic meter in English. Norse meters rely on alliteration of stressed syllables, a feature which works because Old Norse had a heavy stress on the first syllable of words. By contrast, modern English has a much more variable stress accent, with stress regularly falling on a non-initial syllable. This makes it hard to write in a meter that focuses on alliteration of stressed syllables, as many readers would likely fail to recognize the words with non-initial stress as alliterative.

Another concern is that English has lost many of the Germanic words that alliterated with each other, and replaced them with loanwords which do not, while many of the Germanic words it has retained have changed their meaning dramatically, making them impossible to use in their original context. This can be seen, for instance, with the Old Norse word *urðr*, "fate". Its English cognate is *weird*, which once also meant "fate" but has evolved to mean "strange". Using this word with its old meaning would be confusing at best and illegible at worst.

These differences can be observed in the following stanza, from the poem *Vøluspá*. The poem is written in *fornyrðislag* "mythic meter", the most common meter for Eddic poetry. This meter works by splitting each line into two half-lines, with each half containing two stressed syllables and two or three unstressed syllables. The first stressed syllable of the second half-line must alliterate with one of the stressed syllables of the first half. Consonants and the clusters *sp-*, *st-*, and *sk-* may only alliterate with examples of the same consonant, while vowels may alliterate with any other vowel. *J* is also considered a vowel for alliterative purposes. For demonstrative purposes, stressed syllables have been bolded:

> **Ár** var **alda** þar er **ekki var**,
> vara **sandr** né **sær** né **sval**ar **unn**ir,
> **jørð fann**sk æva né **upphim**inn,
> **gap** var **ginn**unga, en **gras hver**gi.

By contrast, English meter commonly relies more on alternating between stressed and unstressed syllables. This book uses various types of iambic meters, which operate on a pattern of alternating unstressed syllables with stressed ones. This can be seen in my blank verse translation of the above stanza, again with stressed syllables in bold:

> I **know** the **first** of **days** when **no**thing **was**;
> there **was** no **sand**, no **sea**, no **freez**ing **waves**,
> there **was** no **earth**, no **hea**vens **high** a**bove**,
> there **was** no **grass**, but **on**ly **gap**ing **void**.

By drawing on the rich poetic tradition of English rather than that of Old Norse, I have (hopefully) been able to produce a translation that captures both the meaning and the poetic flair of the original texts without relying on outdated vocabulary or resorting to prose. Indeed, many translators of other works before me seem to have felt similarly; the Homeric epics, the *Aeneid*, and even the Old English poem *Beowulf* have all received blank verse translations in the past, but as far as I am aware, the *Poetic Edda* has never been translated in this way.

That said, in honor of the originals, I have gone out of my way to include alliteration where the meter allows for it. Also, since Norse names have only been lightly Romanized, it bears mentioning that the letter Þ/þ is pronounced like the *th* in *think*, while ð is like the *th* in *that*.

A final note: I am fully aware that many bigoted people and organizations have attempted to appropriate Norse literature and cultural symbols in order to advance prejudiced views regarding race, gender, and other cultural topics. I wholeheartedly condemn, and neither have, nor desire any form of association with, these individuals and groups, and maintain that anyone, no matter their blood or background, can appreciate the beauty and wisdom found in the literature of the old North.

An Overview of the Norse Pantheon

As many readers will be aware, the Norse were a polytheistic people, and worshipped a broad array of gods and goddesses. These gods were split into two tribes: the Aesir, the primarily worshipped group who live in the land of Asgarð, and the more obscure Vanir, denizens of Vanaheim. Unlike the Greek and Roman gods, the Norse deities do not fit strictly into "god/goddess of X" categories, but certainly do have domains with which they were associated, domains which sometimes overlapped. The primary deities include:

- Oðin: Probably the most important Norse god, the son of the fiends Bor and Bestla, associated with war, death, wisdom, magic, poetry, runic writing, and kingship. He famously gathers half those killed in battle every day and takes them to his hall, Valhalla, where they fight, feast, and drink until they ride into battle at the end of the world. At Ragnarok, he will face the monstrous wolf Fenrir, and will be defeated and swallowed whole.

- Þor: Son of Oðin and the personified Earth, associated with storms, valor, and sacred protection. He is the guardian of humankind, and defends them from devils and trolls with his hammer, Mjolnir, and these battles were believed to cause thunder and lightning. His wife is Sif, and his sons are Magni and Moði. At Ragnarok, he will battle and kill the massive snake Jormungand, but then be killed by its venom.

- Loki: A devious trickster god, son of the fiends Farbauti and Laufey, and blood brother to Oðin. His wife is Sigyn, and he also fathered Hel, Fenrir and Jormungand with the devil woman Angrboða. His exact religious role is unclear, but in mythology he was credited with the creation of fishing nets, and was associated with mirages and cobwebs. After angering the gods (exactly how varies), he is chained to a rock with a snake above him, dripping poison into his eyes. He remains chained till Ragnarok, where he is killed by Heimdall.

- Frey: A god associated with rulership, peace, light, and male sexuality. The son of Njorð and his unnamed wife, he was originally one of the Vanir, and was sent to the Aesir as a hostage after their conflict. His wife is Gerð, who he gained at the cost of his magic sword; without it, he will be overwhelmed and killed by the flame-devil Surt at Ragnarok.

- Freyja: The most prominent of the Norse goddesses, associated with love, beauty, magic, and female sexuality. She is the twin sister of Frey, and thus also daughter to Njorð. Though she is married to a rather obscure figure named Oð, her promiscuity is probably her most-mentioned trait in the surviving sources. She also claims half of those killed in battle and takes them to her hall of Folkvang.

- Njorð: A god associated with the wind and sea. He was originally one of the Vanir, and was sent with his two children to the Aesir as a hostage after the end of the war between them. He fathered Frey and Freyja with his sister, but after joining the Aesir was unhappily married to Skaði.

- Frigg: Wife of Oðin, and mother to their sons Baldr and Hoð. She is a domestic goddess associated with marriage, weaving, childbirth, and prophecy.

- Tyr: A god associated with war and justice, who depending on the source is either the son of Oðin or the devil Hymir. He is most well-known for having lost one of his arms to the wolf Fenrir, as a price for chaining him. At Ragnarok, he will battle Garm, the dog who guards Hel's realm, and the two will kill each other.

- Baldr: The son of Oðin and Frigg, associated with light and virtue. Frigg made him invulnerable to most things, overlooking only mistletoe; upon discovering this, Loki tricks his blind brother Hoð into murdering him with a spear made of it.

- Heimdall: The gods' watchman, who shields Asgarð from incursions. He is the son of nine mothers, and was believed to have fathered the different social classes. At Ragnarok, he will blow his horn, Gjallarhorn, whose sounds will be heard everywhere, and this will mark the beginning of the end. He will be killed by Loki in the final battle.

- Skaði: A goddess associated with winter, mountains, and skiiing. Originally one of the devils, she is the daughter of Þjazi. She received land and Njorð's hand in marriage as compensation for her father's death.

- Bragi: A minor god associated with poetry, especially the more complex poetic systems employed by Norse skalds.

- Iðun: A minor goddess, wife of Bragi. She keeps apples that grant the Aesir eternal youth, may have been associated with youth.

- Honir: A minor god associated with prophecy, closely associated with Oðin and Loki. He was sent as a hostage to the Vanir after their war with the Aesir, ostensibly for his leadership skills. However, he tended to defer to Mimir on matters of leadership.

- Mimir: One of the Aesir, renowned for his wisdom. He was sent as a hostage to the Vanir after their war with the Aesir, and often made leadership decisions on behalf of the disinterested Honir. Enraged by this, the Vanir decapitated him and sent his head to Oðin, who bound it with necromantic magic so he could still hear Mimir's wisdom.

- Ull: A minor god who appears to have once had great prominence. He is the son of Þor's wife Sif from a previous relationship, and is associated with archery, hunting, and skiing. He was also called on for protection in duels.

The gods are opposed by the *jotnar*, another tribe of gods associated with chaos, destruction, and other calamities, who dwell in the realm of Jotunheim. The name *jotnar* has been traditionally (and misleadingly) translated as "giants", a fumbling attempt by 19th-century scholars to associate them with the *gigantes* of Greek myth. While these two groups share the quality of being the gods' enemies, the *jotnar* are not any larger than the gods or humans, as the name "giant" might imply. The most literal translation possible is "eater", while I have rendered the word with the more poetic rendering of "devil" or "fiend", which emphasizes their role as enemies of the gods without misleading anyone as to their size. Prominent *jotnar* include:

- Ymir: The first being to ever exist, father of all gods and devils, born from the intersection of ice and fire in the primeval void of Ginnungagap. He was killed by Oðin and his brothers, and his corpse used to create Miðgarð, the world of humans.

- Hel: Daughter of Loki and Angrboða, cast into the frozen land of Niflheim by Oðin at birth. There she built a hall, named after herself, which is the destination of all those who die of sickness and old age.

- Fenrir: A massive wolf, son of Loki and Angrboða. The gods chained him out of fear of his might, with Tyr losing his hand in the process. He will remain chained until Ragnarok, where he will lead the devils into battle. There he will swallow Oðin whole, but be killed by Oðin's son, Viðar.

- Jormungand: An enormous snake, son of Loki and Angrboða. He lives in the ocean to the edge of the world, and his length surrounds the entire Earth. He will face Þor at Ragnarok, where the god will kill him.

- Ægir: A devil associated with the sea. He hosts massive feasts in his hall for the gods. His wife, Ran, is a goddess associated with drowning.

- Þjazi: Father of Skaði, who once kidnapped Iðun and stole her apples. The gods were narrowly able to recover Iðun and kill Þjazi, and placed his eyes in the sky as stars.

Though the Norse believed in many gods, there was one power they held higher than any of them: fate. Fate was believed to be fixed at one's birth, and to be both immutable and unknowable. Bravery in the face of an unchanging destiny was a greatly respected trait among the Norse, and is a major theme of the *Poetic Edda*.

Mythological Poems
Tales of the Gods, Elves, and Fiends

Vøluspá

The Seer's Prophecy

Introduction

Probably the most famous poem of the entire Edda, *Vǫluspá* "The Seer's Prophecy" is preserved in two manuscripts: as the first poem of the *Codex Regius,* and also in the 14th-century *Hauksbók*. It is also quoted extensively in the *Prose Edda*, from which it gets its modern title. These sources differ quite markedly from each other, and the poem here is a synthesis of the two manuscript versions.

As its title indicates, the poem's plot details a prophecy by a *vǫlva*, a female seeress, delivered to the god Oðin, detailing the creation and destruction of the world, the events leading to the rise and fall of the Norse pantheon, the famous *ragnarøk* ("judgment of the gods", not "twilight of the gods", as it has been commonly mistranslated), and finally the world's rebirth as a lush paradise.

The dating of this poem has also proven among the most controversial of Eddic poems. It is likely Icelandic in origin, as its descriptions of the sun turning black and the sky turning red closely mirror the effects of a volcanic eruption. The true controversy has come from what appear to be signs of Christian influence on the poem; the aforementioned "judgment", the cleansing and renewal of a flawed world mirroring the Christian Judgment Day, the torture of sinners by the dragon Niðhogg, and one *Hauksbók*-exclusive stanza, which describes a "mighty one" descending to rule the new world, in what seems to be a vague reference to Jesus. These apparent Christianisms in an otherwise pagan poem may suggest a composition date close to Iceland's 999 conversion to Christianity, perhaps in the late 900s or early 1000s.

1.   I ask for hearing from the holy ones,
and all of Heimdall's sons,[1] the high and low!
For Valfoðr would hear the tales I know
of ancient things that happened long ago.

2.   I know the devils born in early days,
the ones who fostered me so long ago.
I know nine worlds, nine women in the wood,
I saw the Measure-Tree beneath the earth.[2]

3.   I know the first of days when nothing was;
there was no sand, no sea, no freezing waves,
there was no earth, no heavens high above,
there was no grass, but only gaping void.

4.   Before the sons of Bor, the mighty ones,
raised mighty Miðgarð from the darkest depths,
the sun began to shine upon the stones,
the ground was overgrown with blooming leeks.

5.   Then came the sun, companion of the moon,
and cast her hand across the heavens' edge.
The sun did not know where to build her hall,
the moon did not know what strength he had,
the stars did not know how to place themselves.

6.   The great assembly of almighty gods
sat in their judgment-seats, and held debate.
They named the night and day, the dusk and dawn,
they named the morning and the afternoon,
arranged the sky, so all could count the years.

7.   The gods then gathered at the Iðavell
and built great halls and temples for themselves.
They lit the forge, and crafted wondrous things,
they crafted tongs and tools of many types.

---

[1] Humans.

[2] Yggdrasil, the world-tree, as a seed beneath the ground.

8. They played the tables in the verdant fields
and did not have the slightest need for gold
until three mighty fiendish ladies came
down from the northern lands of Jotunheim.

9. The great assembly of almighty gods
sat in their judgment-seats, and held debate.
They chose the one to make a host of dwarves
from bloody sea and bluish, rotten rocks.

10. They made Moðsognir chief of all the dwarves,
and he had Durin serve as his right hand.
Within the earth the dwarves made shapes of men
from rock and stone, as Durin told them so.

11. They fashioned North and South and East and West,
and Nyi, Niði, Alþjof, Dvalin, Nain,
and Nori, Nar and Niping, Dain as well,
and Bivor, Bavor, Bombur, Anar, An,
Mjoðvitnir and Ai, and many more they made.

12. Like Fili, Kili, Fundin, Nali too,
and Hepti, Vili, Hanar, Sviur and Svið,
and Billing, Bruni, Buri, Bild, Fornbogi,
and Frar and Fraeg and Loni, Jari, too,
and Aurvang, also Eikinskjaldi.

13. and Veig and Gandalf, Vindalf, Þrain and Þror,
and Þorin, also Þrekk and Vit and Lit,
and Ny and Nyrað, Raðsvið, Regin too,
and that's the list of all the dwarves they made.

14. Except the dwarves in Dvalin's company,
the line of kin with Lofar at the end.
They traveled forth from out of stony halls
through Joruvell to Aurvang's muddy home.

15. Their names were Draupnir, Har, and Dolgþrasir
and Gloin, Hlevang, Haugspori as well,
and Skirvir, Virvir, Skafið, also Ai,

16.   and Alf and Yngvi, Eikinsjaldi again,
        then Fjalar, Frosti, Finn and Ginnar last.
        The list of Lofar's kin will be recalled
        as long as there are living things alive.

17.   Until three wise and mighty gods came out
        and wandered far along the sandy shore.
        And there they found, without a form or fate,
        a pair of trees, and named them Ash and Elm.

18.   They had no breath, they had no mind, no spirit,
        they had no flesh, no voice, no handsome looks,
        so Oðin gave them breath, and Honir spirit,
        and Loður flesh and voice and handsome looks.

19.   I know an ash, its name is Yggdrasil,
        a lofty tree that's splashed with pearly clay.
        It spawns the dew that scatters in the dales
        and stands, forever green, above the well of fate.

20.   I know the three omniscient ones who rose
        out of the sea that flows beneath the tree.
        The first is Urð, the second Verðandi,
        the third is Skuld; and then they carved on sticks
        the laws of fate, the births and deaths of men,
        and set the destinies of everyone.

21.   I know the war, the first that ever was,
        that came when Gullveig was impaled on spears
        and burned three times within the High One's hall.
        Three times she burned, three times she rose again,
        she suffered much, and yet she never died.

22.   They called her Heið when she would come to homes,
        she captured spirits, told of things to come,
        she cast her magic everywhere she could,
        she was the greatest joy of evil brides.

23.   Then Oðin flung his spear into the host
        to fight the war, the first that ever was.
        But Asgarð's walls were smashed to tiny bits,
        the Vanir strode amidst the holy halls.

24.   The great assembly of almighty gods
        sat in their judgment-seats, and held debate
        to choose if they should pay a hefty price
        or all the gods should offerings receive.

25.   The great assembly of almighty gods
        sat in their judgment-seats, and held debate
        to learn who mixed deception in the air
        and how the wife of Oð was pledged to fiends.

26.   Alone struck Þor, his face stained red with rage,
        he could not stand aside for these events!
        Their oaths were broken, and their binding words,
        as was the trust of all of Jotunheim.[3]

27.   I know where Heimdall's hearing[4] hides, beneath
        the holy tree that does not want for light.
        I know the stream that splashes in the mud
        from Oðin's pledge.[5] Have I yet told enough?

28.   I know of Baldr, bloody sacrifice,
        the son of Oðin, he of hidden fate,
        of how there stood, full-grown, above the fields,
        the slender, lovely little mistletoe.

29.   How from that tree, which seemed no harm at all,
        poor Hoð once flung a single deadly spear!
        How Baldr's brother, born in just a day,
        avenged him after but a night of life.

30.   He never got to bathe or comb his hair
        before he brought his brother to the flame,
        And Frigg cried out and wept in Fensalir
        for Valhall's loss. Have I yet told enough?

---

[3] A reference to a story also told by Snorri, where the gods offered Freyja as payment to a
devil for repairing Asgarð's wall, only for Þor to kill him instead.
[4] His ear.
[5] His eye, left in the well as a price for its wisdom.

31.   I know of Loki, bound beneath the grove
        of steaming springs by Narfi's guts and gore.
        There Sigyn, joyless, shields her husband's face
        from serpent spit. Have I yet told enough?

32.   I sat outside, alone, when Oðin came,[6]
        the Frightful One peered deep into my eyes,
        "What do you want from me? What's with these tests?
        I know it all, the place you hid your eye,
        you sank it deep in Mimir's famous well.
        Each morning Mimir drinks the finest mead
        from Oðin's pledge!" Have I yet told enough?

33.   Then Herjafoðr brought me rings and torcs,[7]
        he gave me wealth and words and seeing-staves,
        so I could stretch my sight to every world.

34.   I saw the valkyries from far and wide
        who all were riding to the realm of gods.
        For Skuld with shield I saw, and Skogul too,
        and Gunn and Gondul, Hild and Geirskogul;
        and all of them are some of Herjan's girls,
        the valkyries who ride along the earth.

35.   I see the eastern stream of blades and swords
        that flows through poisoned dales; its name is SliÞ.

36.   I see there stands up north in Niðavoll
        a golden hall, the home of Sindri's kin.
        I see there, standing proud in Okolnir,
        the ale-hall of the devil called Brimir.

37.   I see a hall that stands in Nastrond, far
        beyond the sun, its entrance facing north.
        Its roof forever rains a poisoned mist,
        its walls are built from many serpents' spines.

---

[6] Germanic seeresses practiced a ritual called *útiseta* "out-sitting", which involved sitting alone at night, often atop barrows, to commune with spirits or deities.

[7] Presumably as payment for a vision of the future, Oðin being impressed by her knowledge of the past.

38.   I see there, flailing in a vicious stream,
a host of liars, thieves, and murderers,
adulterers, and those who broke their oaths.
I see how Niðhogg drains them of their blood,
and wolves tear off their flesh. Would you hear more?

39.   The old one[8] lives in Jarnvið, to the east
and there she raises Fenrir's litter well.
A certain she-wolf from that mighty brood
is called the troll-shaped stalker of the moon.

40.   She gladly fills her gut with dead mens' flesh
and stains the halls of heaven red with blood.
The sun will darken in the days to come
and cold will reign. Have I yet told enough?

41.   The devils' happy herdsman, Eggþer, will
sit on a barrow and will play his harp.
Then high above him, in the gallows-tree,
the ruddy rooster Fjallar first will crow.

42.   Then Gullinkamb, the rooster of the gods,
will crow, and Herjafoðr's host will stir.
Then last a third will crow beneath the earth,
and wake the dead within the halls of Hel.

43.   Then Garm will howl before the gates of hell,
the chains will break, and free the greedy wolf!
I see so much, and I can tell you more
about the bitter judgment of the gods.

44.   Brothers will fight and spill each other's blood,
the bonds of kin will break and never mend.
The world will be a vicious land of whores
where earth will scream and witches freely fly,
a time of axes, blades, and broken shields,
of savage winds and savage men; there'll be
no love or mercy when the world will fall.

---

[8] Some sort of female devil. The litter she raises are monstrous wolves, not necessarily
Fenrir's children.

45.   Then Mimir's sons will play, and fate will spin
when Gjallarhorn's resounding roar is heard.
The horn will rise, and Heimdall loudly blow,
and Mimir's head will share its mind with Oðin.

46.   Then Yggdrasil will tremble where it stands,
the ancient ash will groan, and free the fiend.[9]
Those on the road to hell will be afraid
before the flames of Surt consume it whole.

47.   How are the mighty gods? How are the elves?
The devils cry for war, the gods hold council.
The dwarves will sigh behind their doors of stone
and rocky walls. Have I yet told enough?

48.   And Garm will howl before the gates of hell,
the chains will break, and free the greedy wolf!
I see so much, and I can tell you more
about the bitter judgment of the gods.

49.   Then Hrym will ride out west, his shield held high,
and Jormungand will writhe with fiendish rage.
The serpent's waves will drown the highest birds,
and set the ship of nails towards the land.

50.   Across the eastern sea the ship will come
with Muspell's host, and Loki at the wheel.
The wolf will lead the devils off to war
while Byleipt's brother brings the fiends to shore.

51.   Then Surt will travel from the south, his flames
destroying trees, his blade as bright as sun.
The rocky cliffs will fall, and witches reel,
mankind will head for hell, the sky will split.

---

[9] Probably Fenrir. Snorri mentions that the quake will break all chains, including the unbreakable one that binds the wolf.

52.   The second sorrow of fair Hlin[10] will come
        when Oðin goes against the swamp-wolf's jaws
        and Beli's slayer[11] faces flaming Surt,
        and when the fragrant love of Frigg will fall.

53.   Then Viðar, son of Sigfaðir, will come
        to face the wolf and earn his just revenge.
        His blade will pierce the heart of Hveðrung's son,
        and thus claim justice for his father's death.

54.   And Garm will howl before the gates of hell,
        the chains will break, and free the greedy wolf.
        I see so much, and I can tell you more
        about the bitter judgment of the gods.

55.   The belt of Earth[12] will gape across the sky,
        his maw will stretch from earth to heaven's heights,
        and Þor alone will face the serpent's might
        as Fenrir is consumed by Viðar's wrath.

56.   The noble son of Hloðyn[13] then will face
        the snake for whom dishonor is no threat.
        The sons of men will flee their homes and steads
        when Miðgarð's hero strikes with righteous rage!
        Nine paces will the son of Fjorgyn step
        until he falls before the serpent's breath.

57.   The sun will blacken, earth will sink again,
        and one by one the stars will disappear.
        The world will burn in Muspell's raging flame,
        the sky will choke in clouds of scalding smoke.

58.   And Garm will howl before the gates of hell,
        the chains will break, and free the greedy wolf!
        I see so much, and I can tell you more
        about the bitter judgment of the gods.

---

[10] From context, another name for Frigg, though Snorri claims her as a separate goddess.
[11] Frey.
[12] Jormungand.
[13] Þor. Hloðyn and Fjorgyn are names for his mother, the Earth.

59.   I see the earth will rise a second time
from darkest depths, now green and flush with life.
I hear the falling water roar, I see
an eagle hunting fish in mountain lakes.

60.   The gods will gather at the Iðavell,
they'll talk about the snake that bound the world,
they'll talk about the bitter doom they faced,
they'll talk about the runes of Fimbultyr.

61.   Then in the grass the gods will find again
the gaming pieces and the golden boards
that they had played with in the first of days.

62.   The fields will sprout without the need for work,
all evil will resolve, and Baldr will return!
Then he and Hoð will govern Oðin's hall
as masters of the slain. Would you hear more?

63.   There Honir will be prophet of the gods
and in the land of mighty wind will dwell
the brothers' sons. Have I yet told enough?

64.   And then a mighty ruler will descend
with holy judgment and a guiding hand.

65.   I see a gilded hall, as lovely as can be,
that stands in Gimle, shining like the sun.
There in that hall the greatest men will live
and they'll know only joy for all their lives.

66.   Until the dragon veiled in shadow flies
down from the northern lands of Niðafjoll;
Niðhogg will come with corpses on his wings,
but now my sight has passed, and I must sink.

Hávamál

The High One's Wisdom

Introduction

Hávamál "The High One's Words" is preserved in full only in the *Codex Regius*, and is by far the longest poem in the entire Edda. Its first stanza is also quoted in the *Prose Edda*, and its eighty-fourth is quoted in the *Frostbrǿðra Saga*. Its seventy-sixth is also echoed in the conclusion to the 10th-century poem *Hákonarmál*.

This poem is distinct from the rest of the collection in being neither an encyclopedia or a narrative, but rather a composition of short wisdom verses attributed to the god Oðin. It is also unique in almost certainly being a blend of what used to be several poems, as indicated by its rather sudden changes in tone and subject matter.

The poem's famous first half has Oðin offer advice for how to conduct oneself in life, advocating moderation, fair treatment of guests, and reciprocal treatment of others. He then goes on a lengthy tangent in which he makes some ethically questionable statements on the fickle, untrustworthy nature of women, and tells tales of his attempts at seduction, then returns to the theme of wisdom verse with a series of stanzas directed to a certain Loddfafnir. The poem then gives an account of Oðin's acquisition of the runes, before finishing with a description of the effects of eighteen magic songs that Oðin knows.

Hávamál's composite nature makes dating the entire poem essentially a fruitless endeavor; some of its verses may be among the oldest in the Edda, and others quite late. However, there is good reason to think the bulk of *Hávamál* is probably on the older side; its latter half contains explicitly heathen religious material, and its moral advice sometimes differs quite starkly from traditional Christian morality.

1.   Before you enter any door,
        be sure to look around,
        you never know if enemies
        are lurking up ahead.

2.   Now hear me, hosts, a guest has come,
        where will you have him sit?
        A man who's waiting on the wood[14]
        is not a patient man.

3.   A guest will need an open flame
        when winter chills their bones.
        They'll also need a meal and clothes
        if they've gone through the peaks.

4.   A host should always give their guests
        a towel and kindly words,
        a friendly smile, if they can,
        and lastly, space to speak.

5.   A traveler needs to use their brain,
        but not so much at home.
        A fool who sits among the wise
        will be a laughingstock.

6.   You should not boast about your smarts
        but keep them to yourself,
        for evil rarely finds the wise
        when they are honored guests.
        You'll never find a better friend
        than wisdom, fairly earned.

7.   When cautious men are at a meal
        they do not speak, but watch,
        with eyes they see, and ears they hear,
        and thus they guard themselves.

---

[14] Apparently, it was customary for guests to wait on a pile of firewood until their hosts
let them in.

8.   A man who's held in high esteem
        will live a joyful life,
        but no one has complete control
        of what's in others' hearts.

9.   A man who's wise and greatly praised
        will live a joyful life,
        but evil counsel often comes
        from someone else's mind.

10.   There's nothing better you can bring
        than wisdom on the road,
        it helps like money helps the poor
        when in a foreign land.

11.   There's nothing better you can bring
        than wisdom on the road.
        The worst thing you can bring along's
        a belly full of beer.

12.   It's not so good to drink a lot
        as you have likely heard.
        The more you drink, the less you think,
        with haste your wits will fade.

13.   It's like a heron stabs your skull,
        and sucks out all your brains!
        It caught me tightest in its grip
        when Gunnloð hosted me.

14.   With Fjalar's girl I got so drunk
        that I could hardly move.
        From that I learned it's best to drink
        if you can keep your mind.

15.   A noble man should always be
        clear-eyed and ever brave.
        They should be filled with joy and cheer
        until their death arrives.

16.   A coward thinks they'll never die
       if they avoid a fight.
       Though spears may spare the flesh of fools,
       old age avoids no man.

17.   A fool will gape when seeing friends,
       and mumble uselessly,
       and when they've had a mug of ale
       they'll show their feeble mind.

18.   A man who's traveled far and wide
       and known all sorts of men
       can judge the ways of those they meet
       if they are not a fool.

19.   Don't get too trashed, but drink a bit,
       speak well or not at all.
       No one who's wise will think you're rude
       if you should sleep at dusk.

20.   A greedy man with no control
       will eat till they are sick.
       The wise will laugh at such a man
       for their great boulder-gut.

21.   A cow knows when it's had enough
       and leaves the grass behind,
       but certain men can never find
       their bellies' boundaries.

22.   An evil wretch with no respect
       will jeer at everything,
       but do not know one thing they should:
       that no one's free of flaws.

23.   A fool will stay awake all night
       and of their troubles think,
       when dawn arrives, they'll be a wreck
       and nothing will be solved.

24.   A fool thinks everyone's their friend
       who laughs along with them,
       they'll never know that wise men speak
       of them with mocking words.

25.   A fool thinks everyone's their friend
       who laughs along with them,
       but they will find when trouble comes
       that none will stand with them.

26.   A fool will think they know it all
       if they remain at home,
        but they will not know what to say
       when others question them.

27.   When fools decide to leave their homes
       it's best they shut their mouths,
       for none will know they lack a brain
       unless they use their words.
       Then all will know, except the fool,
       their mouth has overflowed.

28.   To ask and answer questions well
       are signs of being wise.
       The wisest men can't hope to flee
       the idle speech of fools.

29.   A fool can never shut their mouth
       and spews their useless crap,
       A rambling tongue with no control
       will bring itself no good.

30.   It's best you not mock friends or kin
       when you're their honored guest.
       Unquestioned men can seem quite wise
       if spotlights they avoid.

31.   It's best that when disputes begin
       a wise man should depart,
       the ones who stay and laugh can't know
       if foes are laughing too.

32. I've found that even faithful friends
   will hurl abuse at feasts,
   for conflict is the way of man
   and even guests will clash.

33. It's best to eat at morning time,
   unless you're seeing friends,
   in that case, best to eat at noon
   or all you'll do is eat.

34. A bad friend's house is hard to reach
   no matter where they live.
   A good friend's house is reached with ease
   if it is near or far.

35. A guest should leave eventually,
   and must not stay too long,
   I've seen that love can turn to hate
   if someone hangs around.

36. A house is good, though it is small,
   at home, we all are lords!
   It's better if you have a bit
   than if you have to beg.

37. A house is good, though it is small,
   at home, we all are lords!
   It's like an arrow through the heart
   to ask for every meal.

38. Do not allow your sword or spear
   to go outside your sight.
   When traveling, you never know
   when you might need a blade.

39. I've never known a man so kind
   they won't accept rewards,
   nor one so flush with gold and gems
   they won't enjoy a gift.

40.   Don't fear to spend the gold you've earned,
       no man should suffer need!
       Your foes may take what loved ones should,
       for sometimes things go bad.

41.   Bring joy to friends with blades or clothes,
       enjoy their gifts in turn,
       for friendship's based on trading gifts,
       at least the good ones are.

42.   Be true to friends for all your days,
       repay their gifts with gifts.
       If they should laugh, then laugh as well,
       and lie if they lie first.

43.   Be true to friends for all your days,
       and to their friends as well,
       but do not call someone a friend
       who's friends with foes of yours.

44.   If you've a friend you know you trust
       and value their respect,
       then talk to them, and give them gifts,
       and see them when you can.

45.   If you've a friend who you mistrust
       but you want something from,
       then give them sweet but lying words
       as payment for their lies.

46.   If you know someone you mistrust,
       and think that they're a snake,
       then don't be rude, and laugh with them,
       repay their gifts with gifts.

47.   When I was young, I wandered far
       without a place to go.
       When I met others, I felt rich,
       for friends are life's delight.

48.   The generous and bold live best
and never worry much,
but cowards quake at everything
and fear to give a gift.

49.   I saw two scarecrows in a field
and gave them all my clothes.
When freshly dressed, they looked like kings,
for naked men are shamed.

50.   Like pines whose bark is stripped away
and needles long have left
are those whose lives are missing love;
What cause have they to live?

51.   The love between false friends will burn
five days, and then go out,
and on the sixth, you'd never know
they ever cared at all.

52.   You need not buy expensive gifts
to earn another's love.
With half a loaf and sour wine
I met my dearest friend.

53.   As tiny seas have tiny shores
do men have tiny minds.
Thus, none are ever fully wise,
but each in their own way.

54.   It's good to have some wisdom, but
you must not be too wise.
The ones who know a lot of things
do not live happy lives.

55.   It's good to have some wisdom, but
you must not be too wise.
A wise man's heart is rarely full
if wisdom's all they have.

56.   It's good to have some wisdom, but
       you must not be too wise.
       Don't try to learn what fate will bring,
       and you will not know pain.

57.   As wood is burned away by flame,
       and fire kindles flame,
       so wisdom comes from speaking much,
       and silence makes a fool.

58.   Do not sleep in if you would gain
       another's life or wealth.
       A sleeping wolf won't catch a sheep,
       nor lazy men success.

59.   If you've no workers, don't sleep in,
       go do your work yourself,
       it's hobbling if you sleep too late,
       the busy gain the gold.

60.   The wise can tell if logs or bark
       are good for walls or roofs
       and likewise, if their wood will last
       for three months or for six.[15]

61.   When you go out, be clothed and fed,
       it need not be the best.
       Don't be ashamed of what you have
       if it works well for you.

62.   As eagles scream and stretch their heads
       when they approach the sea,
       do those who get in trouble and
       have none to stand with them.

63.   Those who are wise and want it known
       should ask and answer both,
       tell one your secrets, never two,
       if three, the world will know.

---

[15] i.e., a wise man has common sense.

64.   A wise man must control themselves
and keep their power chained.
For they will see, when passions clash,
that strength is often matched.

65.   The two will always kill the one,
the tongue will kill the head,
for men are often paid in kind
for what they say aloud.

66.   I've been too early many times,
and other times too late,
the beer was gone, or not yet done,
the hated aren't on time.

67.   I've often been invited back
when I had little food,
and often friends would have two steaks
when I had eaten one.

68.   The things that humans love are flame
and early morning sun,
a healthy body, if it holds,
and virtue most of all.

69.   A sick man's not an evil man,
some may be blessed with kin,
or some with friends, or some with gold,
or some with character.

70.   I'd rather be alive than not,
the live alone can live,
I saw a rich man's hearth aflame,
but he was dead outside.

71.   A cripple still can ride or drive,
a deaf man still can fight.
I'd sooner lose my sight than life,
a corpse can't do a thing.

72.   I knew two men who once were rich,
       but now they beg for scraps.
       For wealth will pass like winking eyes
       and is a faithless friend.

73.   An empty-headed fool won't know
       how wealth can twist the mind.
       Some men are rich, and others poor;
       that's not the poor man's fault.

74.   I've seen when fools gain wealth and fame
       and women at their side,
       they don't grow wiser, just more proud,
       and into folly charge.

75.   It's good to have a child, though
       you may not live to meet,
       for you'll need kin to raise a stone
       that keeps your name alive.

76.   For cattle die, and kinsmen die,
       and you will die as well.
       A noble name will never die
       if it is truly earned.

77.   For cattle die, and kinsmen die,
       and you will die as well.
       I know one thing that never dies:
       and that's a dead man's deeds.

78.   Speak well of days when night has come,
       of wives when they've been burnt,
       of swords when they've been proven sharp,
       of ice when it's been crossed,
       of beer when it's been drunk.

79.   We drink our ale by fire's heat,
       and only skate on ice,
       We buy our horses when they're thin,
       and filthy blades as well,
       We feed our horses at our homes,
       at friends' we feed their dogs.

80.   It's best to fell a tree in wind,
but sail when there is none.
Go see a lady after dark,
the day has many eyes.
A ship can take you far and fast,
a shield will keep you whole,
a sword will kill your enemies,
a girl can kiss you well.

81.   But do not trust a woman's words
or what she seems to think,
their minds were made on whirling wheels,[16]
their hearts are full of lies.

82.   A woman's lying love is like
a spikeless horse on ice,
a two-year old who thinks they're wise,
a steerless ship in wind,
a reindeer hunter with no limbs
upon a thawing peak,

83.   a broken bow, a burning flame,
the howls of wolves and crows,
a rootless tree, a surging wave,
a pig before the pot,

84.   a flying arrow, coiled snakes,
or ice that's one night old,
a broken blade, a playful cub,
or women's pillow-talk,

85.   a prophet's words, a wounded calf,
a slave who thinks they're free,

86.   or fields whose crops are sown too soon
or babies on the throne,
for weather rules a field's results
and children have no sense.

---

[16] A poetic term for the moon, implying women's minds change like the moon's phases.

87.   Your brother's killer, on the street,
would get no faith from you,
you wouldn't live in half-burnt homes
or ride a crippled horse,
there's never been a fool so great
he'd place his faith in these!

88.   I must be honest, for I know
that men are hardly better.
Our sweetest words are laced with lies,
and thus are women tricked.

89.   We must use gold and honeyed words
to win a woman's love,
and always give her body praise,
for he who woos will win.

90.   Do not find fault with anyone
that's caught in love's embrace,
for beauty can ensnare the wise
where fools might pass it by.

91.   Do not cast blame on anyone
for that which strikes us all.
The wise are oft reduced to fools
by love's enthralling might.

92.   The mind alone can know the heart,
alone one knows oneself.
The wise know there is nothing worse
than being pleased with nothing.

93.   I learned that when in reeds I sat
till I could see my love,
I thought she was my heart and soul
but she thought me a pain.

94.   A body like the morning sun
        did Billing's daughter[17] have,
        I wanted neither fame nor land,
        I only wanted her.

95.   "Oh, Oðin, please come back tonight
        and I will treat you right,
        If others knew we'd shared a bed
        it'd bring my family shame."

96.   And thus deceived, I went back home
        my heart now filled with lust,
        I thought for sure that I would have
        her body and her love.

97.   The first time I came by that night
        the guards were all awake.
        Their torches lit up every path,
        I could not get to her.

98.   I came again before the dawn
        and found the guards asleep.
        Her bed was empty, save a dog
        she'd tied upon the post.

99.   When you know women, you will see
        they view us men as toys,
        that night, I learned this when I tried
        to get into her bed,
        my efforts brought me only shame,
        and not the joy I'd hoped.

100.   You should be happy in your home,
        and generous to your guests,
        Iif wisdom's what you seek, speak well,
        not little or too much,
        a man who cannot speak's a fool,
        for silence is their way.

---

[17] Attested nowhere else, though her father is listed in *Vøluspá* as a dwarf.

101. I've come and gone from Jotunheim,
my tongue there served me well!
It was with words I won my prize
in Suttung's mountain home.

102. My auger cut for me a path
and swallowed all the rock,
the devils' roads stood on all sides,
I could have lost my head.

103. Then Gunnloð on her golden throne
gave me the poets' mead.
She loved me well, and yet she got
a rather poor reward.

104. I earned my wisdom through deceit
and it has served me well,
for poetry, from Oðrerir,[18]
I shared with humankind.

105. I'd never have returned alive
from out of Jotunheim
if not for Gunnloð, kind and fair,
who slept three nights with me.

106. Then after that the devils came
to see me in my hall,
they asked if Evil-Doer came
or if Suttung had killed him.

107. "Oðin," they said, "you swore on rings,
how can we trust your word?
You robbed poor Suttung of his mead
and then made Gunnloð cry."

---

[18] The vat which contained the magical mead that gave Oðin mastery of poetry.

108.   I once went to the sage's seat
        beside the well of fate.
        I did not speak, but only heard
        of runes and Oðin's wisdom.
        And there, within the High One's hall,
        I heard it said like this:

109.   Loddfafnir, hear my wise advice,
        for it will serve you well!
        Sleep all night long, except to piss
        or if you're on patrol.

110.   Loddfafnir, hear my wise advice,
        for it will serve you well!
        Don't sleep with magic-using girls
        or they will steal your mind.

111.   Her spells will take away your love
        for food and drink and friends.
        You'll have no care for laws or deeds,
        you'll live your life depressed.

112.   Loddfafnir, hear my wise advice,
        for it will serve you well!
        Don't love the wives of other men
        or bring them to your bed.

113.   Loddfafnir, hear my wise advice,
        for it will serve you well!
        If you must travel far away,
        make sure you're stocked with food.

114.   Loddfafnir, hear my wise advice,
        for it will serve you well!
        Don't tell an evil man your pains,
        that brings to you no good,
        for evil men will not reward
        your trust with friendly deeds.

115.   You'll never gain a good reward
       for trusting evil men,
       but good men make your name revered
       by virtue of their praise.

116.   I've seen a woman's evil words
       tear off a good man's head.
       Her lying tongue led him to death
       and yet her words were false.

117.   Loddfafnir, hear my wise advice,
       for it will serve you well!
       If you've a friend, someone you trust,
       go see them when you can.
       For roads that no one travels on
       will fill with brush and thorns.

118.   Loddfafnir, hear my wise advice,
       for it will serve you well!
       Find noble friends while you're alive,
       make sure your name is praised.

119.   Loddfafnir, hear my wise advice,
       for it will serve you well!
       Don't ever be the one to end
       a happy friendship, for
       your heart will rot if you cannot
       share minds with anyone.

120.   Loddfafnir, hear my wise advice,
       for it will serve you well!
       Don't waste your words on stupid apes,
       they'll only numb your brain.

121.   The love of friends is best revealed
       when they exchange their minds.
       There's nothing worse than fickle friends
       whose words are only sweet.

122.   Loddfafnir, hear my wise advice,
for it will serve you well!
Don't waste your strength on evil men
or even nasty words,
for noble men will often fail
when evil men attack.

123.   Loddfafnir, hear my wise advice,
for it will serve you well!
Do not make shoes or shafts for spears
unless they're for yourself.
If they have holes or break too fast,
then men will curse your name.

124.   Loddfafnir, hear my wise advice,
for it will serve you well!
If you see evil, name it such,
don't give your foes a break.

125.   Loddfafnir, hear my wise advice,
for it will serve you well!
Do not find joy from evil things,
be pleased alone by good.

126.   Loddfafnir, hear my wise advice,
for it will serve you well!
Do not look up when combat comes
or you'll be driven mad.[19]

127.   Loddfafnir, hear my wise advice,
for it will serve you well!
To fairly earn a woman's love
or get her into bed,
then swear good oaths, and keep to them,
for good men aren't despised.

---

[19] This superstition is more typical of Celtic cultures, suggesting a late stanza probably composed under Irish influence.

128. Loddfafnir, hear my wise advice,
for it will serve you well!
Don't be a coward, but be cautious,
especially with booze,
and married women too,
and thieves who want your stuff.

129. Loddfafnir, hear my wise advice,
for it will serve you well!
Do not mock guests or travelers,
or anyone you meet.

130. You never know what sort of man
has crossed his path with yours.
There's never been a flawless man,
nor a pure evil one.

131. Loddfafnir, hear my wise advice,
for it will serve you well!
Do not ignore a grey-beard's words,
for wise men oft are old.
Good thoughts can come from shriveled bags
that dangle in the wind.

132. Loddfafnir, hear my wise advice,
for it will serve you well!
Don't shout at guests or chase them off,
be sure the poor can eat.

133. A door that's always opening
must have a heavy frame.
Give little gifts when guests depart
or they will curse your name.

134. [20] Loddfafnir, hear my wise advice,
for it will serve you well!
Use earth to guard yourself from beer
and flame to keep you whole.
Use oak to make your bowels move
and corn to stop a spell.
The old can stop a bitter fight,
for hatred use the moon,
use worms to heal a creature's bite,
for evil use the runes.

135. I'll warn you, when you use the runes
the gods have given men,
for which the Mighty Elder suffered long,
and then he painted red,
you'd best not waste your words.

136. Nine days upon a windy tree
and nine long nights I hung!
In Oðin's name I speared my side,
myself in my own name,
upon the tree whose roots run deep,
whose end is known by none.

137. I had no food or drinking horn
until I got the runes.
I learned their names and many forms
then, screaming, I fell back.

138. From Bolþor's son, fair Bestla's dad,
I learned nine mighty songs,
and from the mead of Oðrerir
I took a precious drink.

139. Thus I became the wisest god,
and thus I sowed my seeds.
All beings sought to hear my words
and know of my great deeds.

---

[20] This stanza likely describes some sort of folk medicine or magic.

140.   You'll find the runes, and many staves,
their magic strong indeed,
the runes that Fimbulþul once carved
and painted red as blood,
the runes the mighty gods then spread
throughout the many realms.

141.   The gods received the mighty runes
from me when I returned,
and Dvalin gave the runes to dwarves,
the elves got them from Dain,
through Asvið they reached Jotunheim,
and some I kept myself.

142.   Do you know how to carve?
Do you know how to read?
Do you know how to paint?
Do you know how to test?
Can you invoke the gods?
Can you bring blood to them?
Can you make sacrifice?
Can you light holy flames?

143.   We'd rather get no offerings
than get too much of one.
A gift must be repaid in turn,
and we do not keep debts.
I gave mankind this warning when
I came back from the tree.

144.   I know a song which queens do not,
nor those of women born.
Its name is *Help*, and it can guard
from hate and pain and sorrow.

145.   I know a second song you'd need
to live a healer's life.[21]

---

[21] The second half of this stanza is missing.

146.   I know a third, which I can use
        if I must stop a foe.
        It blunts the edges of their blades
        so they can't hurt a thing.

147.   I know a fourth, I use it when
        my arms and legs are bound.
        My singing breaks the chains and clasps
        and thus my limbs are freed.

148.   I know a fifth, which I can use
        if arrows come my way.
        I slow it till my eyes can see it,
        and thus I can't be harmed.

149.   I know a sixth, if wounds are carved
        for me on sturdy roots,
        The wounds will come to him as well
        and he'll be hurt, not me.

150.   I know a seventh song, when there's
        a hall engulfed in flame,
        This song can save it, even if
        the flame is burning bright.

151.   I know an eighth, it's good to know,
        for it can settle hate
        before it leads to spilling blood,
        this song's spared many lives.

152.   I know a ninth, which I can use
        to keep my ship afloat.
        It calms the wind, it calms the waves
        and lulls the sea to sleep.

153.   I know a tenth, which I can use
        when witches cause me ill.
        It keeps their souls from coming home,
        and thus it breaks their spells.

154.　When my dear friends go off to fight
I sing my eleventh song.
It keeps their shields and armor strong
so they can come home safe.

155.　If I see dangling by the neck
a hanged man in a tree,
my twelfth song wakes them from their sleep
so they can talk to me.

156.　When I must soak a young man's head
before he goes to war,
My thirteenth song will keep him safe
from arrows, blades, and spears.

157.　If I must say before a group
the names of gods and elves,
my fourteenth song contains them all,
let's see a fool do that.

158.　My fifteenth song I got from dwarves
before their doors of stone.
It gives me elven bravery
and godly strength and Oðin's mind.

159.　My sixteenth song can lure a girl
into my arms and bed.
It makes her heart and mind belong
to me and me alone.

160.　If I'm afraid my girl will leave,
I'll sing my seventeenth.
Loddfafnir, you should learn these songs
for they will serve you well.

161.　I'll never teach my eighteenth song
to girls or someone's wife.
I'll only teach it to my sister
or those who love me well.
Some things are better never shared,
so this is my last song.

162.   The High One thus has shared his words
        and wisdom in his hall!
        May they be useful to mankind
        and useless to mankind!
        May he who spoke be greatly blessed,
        and all who heard as well!
        And blessings on the ones who learn
        from anything they heard!

Vafþrúðnismál

The Wisdom of Oðin and Vafþruðnir

Introduction

The poem *Vafþrúðnismál* "The Words of the Great Weaver" is the first of several Eddic poems serving more as a compendium of information than a cohesive narrative. It is preserved both in the *Codex Regius* in its entirety and a fragmentary 14th-century manuscript elegantly titled AM 748 I 4to, minus its first 19 stanzas. It is also extensively quoted in the *Prose Edda*, though oddly Snorri never names the poem.

As mentioned, this poem is essentially an encyclopedia of information about the world as Norse pagans saw it, held together by a simple frame story of Oðin seeking to compare his wisdom with that of the fiend Vafþruðnir.

The date of this poem's composition is uncertain. Nothing in it marks it as especially early or late, though it likely predates the Christianization of Iceland; it is hard to imagine a Christian poet composing a poem of this nature.

Oðin said:

1. "My darling Frigg, I need advice:
I'd like to visit Vafþruðnir
and test the wisdom I have gained
against the wisest fiend of all!"

Frigg said:

3. "My darling Oðin, stay at home
and keep away from Vafþruðnir!
Of all the sons of Jotunheim
he is by far the mightiest!"

Oðin said:

4. "I've traveled far and wandered wide
and gained the wisdom of the worlds,
I'd like to see how Vafþruðnir,
the wisest devil, keeps his home."

Frigg said:

5. "Then travel safe, and come home safe,
and be a generous guest to him!
May wisdom be your sword and shield
if you must clash with Vafþruðnir!"

6. So Oðin left to test his mind
against the all-wise Vafþruðnir.
At last he reached the devil's hall,
he pushed the doors apart, and said,

7. "Vafþruðnir, hail! I've traveled far
to meet you and to see your hall!
I want to know if you are wise
or if you merely know a lot!"

Vafþruðnir said:

8. "What sort of man comes barging in
and hurls such language at his host?
I'll tell you now, you won't depart
unless your wisdom matches mine!"

Oðin said:

9.   "And by the way, I'm Gagnrað,
I'm thirsty from my journey here!
Don't be a stingy host to me,
go get your guest a horn to drink!"

Vafþruðnir said:

10.   "Then don't stand yapping at the door,
come in, sit down, and have a drink!
Then we shall see who's wiser here,
the devil or his foolish guest."

Oðin said:

11.   "When you're a guest in someone's home,
you should speak well, or not at all.
A rambling tongue will be no help
if I'm to face a frosty fiend."

Vafþruðnir said:

12.   "All right then, Gagnrað, let's see
if you're in fact as wise as me!
So tell me, what's the horse's name
who bears the sun across the sky?"

Oðin said:

13.   "Skinfaxi is the horse's name
who pulls the sun across the sky.
The Goths say he's the greatest horse,
his mane is always shining bright."

Vafþruðnir said:

14.   "All right then, Gagnrað, let's see
if you're in fact as wise as me!
What is the horse's name who hauls
the night from east to west?"

Oðin said:

15.   "Hrimfaxi is the horse's name
who drags the night above the gods.
And from his mane fall drops of dew
that mortals find at morning-time."

Vafþruðnir said:

16.   "All right then, Gagnrað, let's see
if you're in fact as wise as me!
What is the river called that splits
the earth between the gods and fiends?"

Oðin said:

17.   "It's Ifing, that's the river's name
which separates the gods and fiends.
Its raging currents always flow,
its waters will not ever freeze."

Vafþruðnir said:

18.   "All right then, Gagnrað, let's see
if you're in fact as wise as me!
What do they call the massive field
where Surt will battle with the gods?"

Oðin said:

19.   "The field where Surt will face the gods
is known as Vigrið everywhere.[22]
Each way it runs a hundred leagues
and only they may stand within."

Vafþruðnir said:

20.   "I see, my guest, in fact you're wise!
Come join me at the table's head,
let's have a drink, and bet our lives
on who's the wiser of us two."

Oðin said:

21.   "Tell me this first, then, if you know,
let's see how wide your wisdom is.
How did the earth and heavens high
first come to be, great Vafþruðnir?"

---

[22] Except to the author of *Fáfniskviða*, who calls this field *Oskopnir*.

Vafþruðnir said:

22.   "The earth was made from Ymir's flesh,
and rocks and mountains from his bones,
his skull was used to make the sky,
his blood gushed out to form the sea.

Oðin said:

23.   "Tell me this second, if you know,
let's see how wide your wisdom is.
How did the Sun and wandering Moon
first come to be, wise Vafþruðnir?"

Vafþruðnir said:

24.   "The father of the Sun and Moon,
I know his name, it's Mundilfari.
Each day they both must turn the sky
so men can count the passing years."

Oðin said:

25.   "If you are wise, you must know this,
the third thing that I want to hear,
who is the father of bright Day
and Night, with all her darkened moons?"

Vafþruðnir said:

26.   "I know that Delling fathered Day,
but it was Norr who sired Night.
They made the Moon grow bright, then dark,
so men could count the passing months."

Oðin said:

27.   "They say you're wise, so let me see
if you can answer this as well,
how did warm Summer and cold Winter
first come to live among the gods?"

Vafþruðnir said:

28.   "Vindsval's the one who birthed the Winter,
and Summer's father is Svasuð.

Oðin said:

29.   "If you're as wise as I have heard,
        then surely you can answer this:
        Who was the first of Ymir's kin
        that came to be in ancient times?"

Vafþruðnir said:

30.   "My kind were made before the earth,
        the first was known as Bergelmir,
        his father's name was Þruðgelmir,
        and Þruðgelmir's was Aurgelmir."

Oðin said:

31.   "You may be wise, but let us see
        if you know what I want to hear:
        If he did not have parents, how
        did Aurgelmir first come to be?"

Vafþruðnir said:

32.   "From icy streams a poisoned cloud
        burst out and grew till he was formed.
        All devils come from poisoned ice,
        that's why my kinsmen all are fierce."

Oðin said:

33.   "Now tell me this, if you are wise,
        then surely you will know,
        exactly how did Aurgelmir
        have sons without a woman there?"

Vafþruðnir said:

34.   "It's said that in his armpit he
        grew for himself a boy and girl,
        and foot by foot he grew himself
        another son, who had six heads."

Oðin said:

35.   "You might be wise, but tell me this,
        you've piqued my curiosity,
        what is the oldest memory
        you have of days before the earth?"

Vafþruðnir said:

36. "The oldest thing I can recall
is Bergelmir's demise.
In ancient days that wisest fiend
was placed upon a mighty mill."

Oðin said:

37. "If you're as wise as I have heard,
then surely you can answer this.
What is the origin of wind
and why is it invisible?"

Vafþruðnir said:

38. "An eagle sits at heaven's edge
named Hraesvelg, born to fiendish kin.
He flaps his wings, and makes the wind
that blows across the earth and sea."

Oðin said:

39. "Now tell me this, if you in fact
know how the gods will meet their fate.
We all know Njorð is widely famed,
but he is not of godly birth,
so how did he first come to Asgarð?"

Vafþruðnir said:

40. "Wise Njorð was born in Vanaheim
and was a hostage to the gods.
And when they all have met their fate
he'll join the Vanir once again."

Oðin said:

41. "Now tell me this, if you in fact
know everything there is to know.
Exactly what does Herjan's host
do as they wait for Heimdall's horn?"

Vafþruðnir said:

42. "They meet in battle every day
within the yard of Oðin's hall.
They choose the slain, then ride away,
and afterwards they sit and feast."

Oðin said:

43.   "The next thing that I'd like to know,
if you are wise enough to share,
exactly how'd you come to know
the secrets of the gods and fiends
and how the threads of fate are spun?"

Vafþruðnir said:

44.   "I've learned these secrets and of fate
by traveling through every world.
I've seen nine worlds that lie beneath
the misty halls of Niflhel,
the home of those who die from hell."

Oðin said:

45.   "I too have traveled far and wide
and gained the wisdom of the worlds.
How will humanity survive
the Fimbulvetr's frigid wind?"[23]

Vafþruðnir said:

46.   "The humans Lif and Lifþrasir
will hide away in Hoddmim's woods.[24]
They'll keep alive with honeydew
and they'll repopulate the world."

Oðin said:

47.   "I too have traveled far and wide
and gained the wisdom of the worlds.
How will the Sun re-light the sky
once Fenrir has consumed her whole?"

Vafþruðnir said:

48.   "The Sun will birth a single girl
before the wolf puts out her light.
And when the gods have met their fate,
she'll ride along her mother's roads."

---

[23] A brutal, three-year winter that precedes the end of the world.
[24] Possibly a kenning for Yggdrasil.

Oðin said:

49.　"I too have traveled far and wide
　　and gained the wisdom of the worlds.
　　Who are the girls that ride across
　　the sea, whose minds are always wise?"

Vafþruðnir said:

50. [25]　"Above Mogþrasir's little town
　　his girls will ride in groups of three.
　　Though they are all of fiendish birth,
　　they'll be the guardians of the world."

Oðin said:

51.　"I too have traveled far and wide
　　and gained the wisdom of the worlds.
　　What gods will rule the world reborn
　　when all the blackened flames have died?"

Vafþruðnir said:

52.　"Viðar and Vali are the gods
　　who'll rule when blackened fires die.
　　The sons of Þor will be the heirs
　　of Mjolnir when the war is done."

Oðin said:

53.　"I too have traveled far and wide
　　and gained the wisdom of the worlds.
　　What will bring Oðin to his death
　　when all the worlds are torn apart?"

Vafþruðnir said:

54.　"The hungry wolf will eat him whole,
　　but Viðar will avenge his death.
　　He'll face the wolf, and cleave his jaws,
　　enraged, he'll stab him in the heart."

---

[25] It's unclear who this stanza refers to.

Oðin said:

55.   "I too have traveled far and wide
and gained the wisdom of the worlds.
When Baldr's corpse was brought to burn,
what words did Oðin say to him?"

Vafþruðnir said:

56.   "I cannot say, for only you
know what you whispered in his ear!
For all my wisdom, I'm a fool,
for you're not Gagnrað, but Oðin!
My wisdom can't compete with yours,
for you're the wisest one of all!"

Baldrs Draumar

Baldr's Dreams

Introduction

Baldrs Draumar "Baldr's Dreams" is a short poem found only in the AM 748 I 4to manuscript. It follows *Hárbarðsljóð* in that manuscript, but I have moved it in with the other poems that focus chiefly on Oðin. AM is also the source of the poem's modern title, but many 17th-century paper copies instead call it *Vegtamskviða* "Vegtam's Poem," and modern editors have sometimes given it this title.

The poem's plot revolves around Oðin's investigation of his son Baldr's nightmares, presumably regarding his impending death, and his journey to the land of the dead in search of answers.

Attempts to date this poem are based mainly on its stylistic similarities with other Eddic poems; its opening stanza is almost exactly the same as *Þrymskviða*'s fourteenth, while its eleventh closely mirrors *Vǫluspá*'s description of Vali's vengeance. Considering the widespread popularity of these two poems, it is a distinct possibility that *Baldrs Draumar* drew from them, which would date it to the late 10th century at the earliest, and possibly as late as rhe 12th.

1. The gods had gathered in a rush,
   the goddesses joined them as well.
   They sat there long, and long they sought
   to find why Baldr dreamed of death.

2. Then up rose Oðin, Man of Ages,
   he saddled Sleipnir up and rode
   to Niflhel, death's cold abode,
   and met a hound that came from hell.

3. Its chest was smeared with blood and gore
   and long it howled at magic's lord.
   The dead-road thundered as he passed,
   until he reached the hall of Hel.

4. He rode beyond the eastern door
   to where an ancient prophet lay.
   He sang a song that raised the witch,
   and, forced to speak, she said these words:

5. "What sort of man would wander here
   and force me up from death's embrace?
   My corpse was soaked in snow and rain
   for many ages, now long past!"

6. "My name is Vegtam, Valtam's son.
   I know of home, I'll hear of hell!
   What guest is coming, that the hall
   is decked in golden finery?"

7. "For Baldr was the mead prepared,
   with shields above its shining vat.
   The gods will tremble at his death.
   I've said enough, I'll speak no more!"

8. "Not yet, for there are many things
   that I still want to hear from you!
   What sort of man could possibly
   take life away from Oðin's son?"

9.   "His brother Hoð will be the one
        who'll pierce his brother through the side
        and bleed the life from Oðin's son.
        I've said enough, I'll speak no more!"

10.   "Not yet, for there are many things
        that I still want to hear from you!
        Who will claim justice for the deed
        and carry Baldr's bane to burn?"

11.   "In western halls will Rind birth Vali.
        He will not wash his hair or bathe,
        at one night old he'll bring the corpse
        of Hoð to roast in pyre's flames.
        I've said enough, I'll speak no more!"

12.   "Not yet, for there are many things
        that I still want to hear from you!
        Who are the girls who'll weep for him
        and cast their pearly hair aloft?"[26]

13.   "I see, you're not the man I thought,
        your name's not Vegtam, it is Oðin!"
        "And you're no prophet, as I thought,
        three fiendish sons were born to you!"

14.   "Ride home now, Oðin, and be proud,
        for none will call on me again
        till Loki breaks his bloody chains
        and sends his son to eat you whole!"

---

[26] The answer is probably "waves", with their "hair" (literally "neck's corner") being their white crests. It's unclear why this question reveals Oðin's identity.

Grímnismál

Grimnir's Speech

Introduction

Grímnismál "The Words of the Masked One" is another encyclopedic poem preserved in its entirety in both the *Codex Regius* and the AM 748 I 4to, following *Vafþrúðnismál* in both manuscripts. Many of its stanzas are also quoted in the *Prose Edda*.

This is the first of many Eddic poems to begin with a prose introduction. These introductions are likely later additions, probably dating to when these poems were first written down. The context they provide would have been unnecessary when these poems were first composed, as their audience would have already been familiar with the oral traditions, and thus the background of these poems. But as the old oral tradition faded and the poems committed to writing, scribes likely felt it necessary to add prose "explainers" detailing the events leading up to the plots of these poems, as readers were now less likely to have familiarity with the old traditions.

Grímnismál, like the other encyclopedic poems, has only a brief frame plot giving a reason for the characters to share their knowledge. In this case, it follows a visit by a disguised Oðin to the Gothic king Geirroð to test his hospitality, only for Oðin to be tortured for his trouble. He then shares his wisdom with Geirroð's son, Agnar, after the boy takes pity on him and gives him water.

Like the other encyclopedic poems, *Grímnismál* likely predates the Christianization of Scandinavia. Its references to the obscure and archaic gods Ull and Forseti suggest that it may be one of the older poems in this collection, possibly as early as the 9th century.

King Hrauðung of the Goths had two sons. One was named Agnar, and the other was named Geirroð. One day, when Agnar was ten and Geirroð was eight, they rowed out with their fishing gear to catch small fish, and the wind pushed them out to sea. In the darkness of the night, they were shipwrecked; they wandered till they found a farmer, and they wintered with him. While his wife took care of Agnar, the farmer took a shine to Geirroð, and taught him much wisdom.

When spring came, the family gave them a boat. Before they left, the farmer met in private with Geirroð. They had a good wind, and returned to the place where they had departed. Geirroð stood at the boat's bow, and he dove off and pushed the boat back out to sea with Agnar still aboard, saying after him "Go where devils will have you!". The ship blew out to sea, and Geirroð returned to his hometown. By this time, his father had passed, and Geirroð was hailed as king. He ruled for many years and was famous for his virtue.

One day, Oðin and Frigg were sitting in Hliðskjalf, and Oðin said "Frigg, look at your Agnar; he lives in a cave and has children with fiends! But my Geirroð is a king, and rules his land well!". And Frigg said back "He's so stingy that he tortures his guests if he thinks they're an inconvenience to him!" Oðin called this a lie, and they made a bet about it.

Frigg sent her handmaid, Fulla, to Geirroð. She warned the king about a wandering magician who was coming to bewitch him. She also told him that he would know this magician by the fact that no dog would attack him. Geirroð was offended that anyone might think him a poor host, but nonetheless he endeavored to arrest any guest who dogs would not attack.

That man soon came. He wore a blue cloak, and called himself Grimnir, but would say nothing else of himself. Geirroð, determined to make him speak, had him placed between two flames, and for eight days and nights he sat and burned between them.

On the ninth night, the flames had progressed such that the cloak on Grimnir's back was burning. Finally, Geirroð's son, named Agnar after his uncle and only ten years old, brought Grimnir a full horn to drink from. He said his father was being dishonorable by arresting and torturing a man who had committed no crime. Grimnir drained the horn, and then said:

1.   "These flames are hot, and burn too fierce,
        please, fire, leave me be!
        My cloak has kept my flesh intact
        but it has burned away.

2.   For eight long days I've roasted here,
        and gained goodwill from none
        except for Agnar, Geirroð's son,
        the boy who'll rule the Goths.

3.   The God of Men will hail you, boy,
        and so you shall be blessed!
        For one small cup no man's received
        a prize so great as this!

4.   I see a holy land that lies
        where gods and elves now dwell.
        I know in Þruðheim Þor will stay
        until he meets the snake.

5.   The land where Ull has built his home
        is known as Ydalir,
        and Alfheim in the first of days
        was teething Frey's reward.

6.   I know a third, where gentle gods
        built halls with silver roofs.
        Its name is Valaskjalf, well-built
        it was in ancient days.

7.   The fourth is known as Sokkvabekk,
        it's lashed with frigid waves.
        There Saga drinks with Oðin gladly
        each day from golden cups.

8.   The fifth is Glaðsheim, Valhall's land,
        it gleams as bright as gold.
        There every day are brought by Hropt
        the weapon-slain he's picked.

9.	Someone who comes to Oðin's hall
	will know it easily.
	Its rafts are spears, its roof is shields,
	its seats are made of mail.

10.	Someone who comes to Oðin's hall
	will know it easily.
	A wolf is hung by the west door,
	an eagle's perched above it.

11.	And Þrymheim is the seventh hall,
	where mighty Þjazi lived,
	but now fair Skaði calls it home,
	and guards her father's lands.

12.	The seventh stead is Breiðablik,
	where Baldr built his hall.
	I know it is the purest land
	where nothing evil lies.

13.	The eighth is Himinbjorg, it's said
	there Heimdall watches all.
	The happy sentry in his hall
	drinks all the finest mead.

14.	The ninth is Folkvang, Freyja's hall,
	where she arranges seats.
	Each day she chooses half the slain
	and Oðin gets the rest.

15.	The tenth is Glitnir, silver-thatched
	and lined with golden poles.
	Forseti[27] lives there all his days
	and there resolves disputes.

16.	The eleventh hall is Noatun,
	where Njorð has built his home.
	the blameless lord of wind and wave
	has built his temples high.

---

[27] Another obscure god, according to Snorri associated with justice.

17.   Grown over with thick brush and grass
        is Viði, Viðar's land.
        on horseback every day he cries
        his father he'll revenge.

18.   Saehrimnir's cooked by Andhrimnir
        each day in Eldhrimnir.
        It is the finest food, but few
        know what Valhalla eats.[28]

19.   But Oðin's always sure to feed
        Geri and Freki too,
        But Herjafoðr lives alone
        on life-sustaining wine.

20.   Hugin and Munin fly each day
        across the boundless earth.
        I fear that Hugin won't return,
        and Munin even more.

21.   The sea roars out, Þjoðvitnir's fish[29]
        lies gladly in its flood.
        Its currents thunder far too strong
        for joyous dead to wade.

22.   The holy gate of Valgrind stands
        upon an open field.
        The gate's so old that no one knows
        how tightly it is locked.

23.   As I recall, Valhalla has
        six hundred forty doors.
        Nine-sixty men will come from each
        to go against the wolf.

---

[28] Saehrimnir is a pig who is slaughtered and cooked each day, and revived the following day. Andhrimnir is Valhalla's cook, and Eldhrimnir is his pot.

[29] Probably Jormungand, the world-snake. *Þjoðvitnir* "wolf of nations" is Fenrir, so his fish must be his brother. Jormungand lives in the sea, so *Þund* must be a name for the sea.

24.   As I recall, Bilskirnir has
        six hundred forty rooms.
        Of every building with a roof,
        the biggest is my son's.

25.   Heiðrun the goat stands by the hall
        and gnaws on Laeraðs limbs.
        She fills a pot with shining mead
        so that there's never none.

26.   The deer Eikþyrnir stands there too
        and gnaws on Laeraðs limbs.
        His horns rain drops in Hvergelmir
        from where all rivers flow.

27.   The Sokin, Eikin, Sið and Við,
        the Gunnþro and the Svol,
        the Fjorm and Fimbulþul as well,
        the Rhine and Rennandi,
        the Gipul, Gopul, Gomul,
        and Geirvimul all flow
        around the hoards of all the gods.

28.   The Þyn, the Vin, the Holl, the Þoll,
        the Grað and Gunnþorin,
        the Dvina, Vegsvinn, Þjoðnuma,
        the Nyt and Not and Nonn,
        the Hronn, the Hrið, the Slið, the Sylg,
        the Ylg, the Gjoll, the Leipt,
        the Við, the Van, the Vond, the Strond.
        These rivers flow near humankind,
        and downwards fall to hell.

29.   The Kormt and Ormt, and Kerlaugs both
        must Þor wade every day
        when he goes to his judgment-seat
        at Yggdrasil the ash
        when flames consume the godly bridge
        and sacred waters seethe.

30.   The gods ride Gyllir, Glað, and Gler
       and Sinir, Skeiðbrimir,
       Falhofnir, Gisl, Silfrintopp,
       and Gulltopp and Lettfeti
       when they go to their judgment-seats
       each day at Yggdrasil.

31.   There are three roots of Yggdrasil
       that run three different ways.
       Hel's under one, the fiends another,
       and men beneath the third.

32.   The squirrel that runs along the tree
       is known as Ratatosk.
       He runs the eagle's insults down
       and then brings Niðhogg's up.

33.   Four stags consume the ash's leaves,
       with necks that face the sky.
       Their names are Dain and Duraþror,
       Duneyr and Dvalin, too.

34.   More snakes lie under Yggdrasil
       than any fool would think.
       The first of them are Goin and Moin,
       the sons of Grafvitnir.
       The rest are Grabak, Ofnir, Svafnir,
       and Grafvolluð as well.
       I think they'll always nibble down
       the roots of Yggdrasil.

35.   That tree does suffer quite a bit,
       much more than men may know.
       Deer eat its leaves, its trunk decays,
       and Niðhogg chews its roots.

36.   That ash is still the best of trees,
        and Skiðblaðnir of ships.
        As Oðin is the best of gods,
        so Sleipnir is of steeds.
        Of bridges is the Bilrost best,
        of skalds is Bragi best.
        As Habrok is the greatest hawk,
        so Garm's the best of dogs,
        and Brimir best of swords.

37.   Ivaldi's sons in ancient days
        did build that best of ships.
        Skiðblaðnir was a gift for Frey,
        the noble son of Njorð.

38.   It's Hrist and Mist who do my will
        and bring me drinking horns,
        and Skeggjold, Skogul, Hild and Þruð
        and Hlokk and Herfjotur
        and Randgrið, Raðgrið, Reginleif
        and Goll and Geirolul
        who bring the beer to champions
        that dwell within my hall.

39.   Arvak and Alsvið, scrawny steeds,
        each morning haul the sun.
        To ease their burden, kindly gods
        put bellows under them.

40.   And Svalin stands before the sun,
        the shining lady's shield.
        The rocks and sea will burn away
        if he should leave his post.

41.   The wolf named Skoll pursues the sun
        to shelter in the trees.
        In front of heaven's burning bride
        runs Hati, Fenrir's son.[30]

---

[30] According to Snorri, Hati chases the moon, and thus runs in front of the sun.

68

42.   The earth was formed from Ymir's flesh,
        the oceans from his blood,
        the rocks, his bones, the trees, his hair,
        and heaven from his skull.

43.   And from his lashes, kindly gods
        made Miðgarð for mankind,
        and from his brain they made the clouds
        and placed them in the sky.

44.   Now Ull and all the rest will bless
        whoever stills the flames.
        For worlds will open over men
        if someone drops the pots.[31]

45.   I've raised my guise before mankind,
        at last, relief shall come.
        For soon I'll join the gods again
        in Aegir's drinking hall.

46.   My names are Grim and Gangleri,
        and Hjalmberi and Herjan, too,
        Þekk and Þriði, Þund and Uð,
        and Helblindi and Har,

47.   and Sað and Svipall, Sanngetall
        and Herteit, Hnikar, too,
        Bileyg, Baleyg, Fjolnir, Bolverker
        and Grimnir, Fjolsvið, Glapsvið,

48.   Siðhott, Siðskegg, Hnikuð, Sigfoðr,
        Atrið, Farmatyr,
        Valfoðr and Alfoðr,
        I've never had a single name
        in any place I've gone.

---

[31] It's unclear from where the pots would be lowered, or why this would do anything.

49.   I'm Grimnir here in Geirroð's hall,
         but Asmund calls me Jalk.
         I'm Kjallar when I draw a sledge,
         at Things I'm Þror, in battle Viður.
         The gods know me as Jafnhar
         and Oski, Omi, Biflindi,
         and Gondlir, Harbarð too.

50.   Sokkmimir called me Sviður once
         and Sviðrir when I hid
         that I alone became the bane
         of Miðviðnir's great son.

51.   For I am Oðin, and I'm Ygg,
         before that, I was Þund.
         Among the gods I'm Vak and Jalk,
         and Gaut and Skilfing, too,
         and Hroptatyr, but some of these
         I came up with myself.

52.   My goodness, Geirroð, you are trashed,
         you're missing much when I'm not here,
         not least of which is Oðin's love!

53.   I taught you much, you never learned,
         your friends have played you false!
         My friend, I see your bloody sword
         will soon lie on the floor!

54.   I'll have your blade-pierced body soon,
         your death is coming fast!
         The disir[32] too are mad at you,
         come at me, if you can!"

King Geirroð sat with his sword on his knee, half-drawn. When he heard that Oðin had come, he rose, hoping to take him down from the fires. He lost his grip on the sword, and it fell hilt-down. The king lost his footing and fell forward, onto the blade, killing him. In that moment, Oðin vanished, and Agnar went on to rule the Goths for many years.

---

[32] Literally *ladies*, a generic term used for goddesses or for female ancestors. Here it likely references the Norns.

Hárbarðsljóð

The Flyting of Þor and Harbarð

Introduction

Hárbarðsljóð "Grey-Beard's Song" is preserved complete in the *Codex Regius* and without its first eighteen stanzas in AM 748 1 4to.

This poem is the first of a few Eddic poems that demonstrate the Germanic tradition of flyting, essentially their equivalent of slam poetry or rap battling. Participants would exchange verses both boasting of their own accomplishments and insulting the other, until one side failed to respond adequately.

The poem's plot deals entirely with its titular flyting, between the god Þor and a boatman named Harbarð (who, as *Grímnismál* helpfully tells us, is Oðin in disguise), as Þor attempts to persuade Harbarð to sail him across a vast fjord.

The poem regularly alternates between various form of meter, as well as some lines of prose, which suggests a poor state of preservation; this, combined with an allusion to this poem's events in a single verse attributed to 10th-century skald Ulf, son of Ugg, suggest an early composition date. However, its linguistic features suggest a date closer to the 11th- or 12th-centuries. A possible explanation is that *Hárbarðsljóð* is a late poem based on older material.

Þor was coming from the east when he came to a fjord. On the other side
was a ferryman with a boat.

Þor yelled:

1. "What boy of boys is standing over there?"

He yelled back:

2. "Who is that grey-beard thundering over there?"

Þor said:

3. "Bring me across the fjord, I'll give you food,
the basket on my back is full of meals!
This morning, when I left, I stuffed my face
with goat and herring meat; I'm still filled up!"

The ferryman said:

4. "You boast of breakfast, not of bravery,
I think you do not know what lies ahead,
your house is ruined, and your mother's dead!"

Þor said:

5. "What sort are you to say such awful things?
No man won't weep that hears his mother's dead!"

The ferryman said:

6. "I think you haven't got three farms to lose!
You have no shoes, you're wearing tattered rags,
I'll bet you've gone commando over there!"

Þor said:

7. "Just bring the boat, I'll show you where to land!
Who owns the ship you're watching over there?"

The ferryman said:

8. "It's Hildolf's boat, he hired me to keep it,
he's very wise, and lives in Raðsey's Sound!
He told me not to ferry vagabonds,
but only noble men and those I know,
so if you want to cross, then say your name!"

Þor said:

9.   "I'm not afraid to give my name it's Þor,
        I'd tell you if I was a criminal!
        I'm Oðin's son, and Meili is my brother,
        Magni and Moði are my noble sons,
        I've given you my name, now tell me yours!"

The ferryman said:

10.   "My name is Harbarð, which I rarely hide!"

Þor said:

11.   "Why hide your name, if you're an upright man?"

Harbarð said:

12.   "If I were not, I'd still defend myself
        from you, unless the Norns have said I'll die!"

Þor said:

13.   "You're lucky it would inconvenience me
        to wet my balls by wading over there!
        I would repay your insolence in kind,
        you brat, if I could get across the fjord!"

Harbarð said:

14.   "Then here I'll stand and wait with bated breath!
        You've met no tougher man since Hrungnir died!

Þor said:

15.   "And now you want to bring up Hrungnir's death!
        His heart was stone, his head was stone as well,
        and yet he could not match me in a fight!

        What were you doing in the meantime, Harbarð?"

Harbarð said:

16.   "I spent five years in Fjolvar's company
        we lived together on the island Algron!
        We fought together, killed their warriors,
        we tested much, and mastered all their girls!"

Þor said:

17.   "So, tell me how it went with all those girls!"

Harbarð said:

18.   "The spunky girls submitted to us both,
the wise ones also were quite kind to us.
They fashioned ropes of sand, and dug the earth
out from the bottom of the deepest dales.
I mastered all of them with scheming wit,
I had all seven sisters in my bed,
and all of them were lusting after me!

What were you doing in the meantime, Þor?"

Þor said:

19.   "I slaughtered Þjazi, mightiest of fiends,
and then I cast his eyes into the sky!
Their light illuminates my bravery,
mankind needs only look above to see it!"

What were you doing in the meantime, Harbarð?"

Harbarð said:

20.   "I was seducing those who ride at night,
I lured them from their husbands, made them mine!
I'd heard that Hlebarð was the strongest fiend,
as tribute I received his mighty wand,
and then I stole his famous wits away!"

Þor said:

21.   "Then you repaid his gift with ill intent."

Harbarð said:

22.   "One oak has bark, the second one may not,[33]
in life we all must watch our own affairs!

What were you doing in the meantime, Þor?

---

[33] An idiom; essentially meaning *you win some, you lose some.*

Þor said:

23.   "I fought the devils in the eastern lands,
        their evil brides who hid away in hills!
        If they had lived, their race would flood the earth,
        they would have taken Miðgarð for their own!

        What were you doing in the meantime, Harbarð?"

Harbarð said:

24.   "I spent some time in Valland, making war,
        I angered princes and ensured no peace!
        For Oðin owns the kings and weapon-slain,
        but Þor owns nothing but the sons of slaves!"

Þor said:

25.   "You'd give the gods unequal shares of men
        as well, if you possessed the power to!"

Harbarð said:

26.   "I see that you are strong, but have no heart,
        in fear you stuffed yourself inside a glove,
        and when that happened, you were hardly Þor!
        Your cowardice was so extreme that you
        were scared to sneeze or fart, lest Fjalar hear!"[34]

Þor said:

27.   "I swear, you bitch, I'd knock your ass to hell,
        if I could get across this fucking fjord!"

Harbarð said:

28.   "Why swing your stick at me? We've no disputes!

        What were you doing in the meantime, Þor?"

---

[34] A reference to a story told by Snorri, where Þor hides from mysterious noises in a hall
which is later revealed to be the glove of a massive devil. Snorri calls this devil Skrymir,
but apparently the composer of this poem knew him as Fjalar.

Þor said:

29.   "In eastern lands I kept the river safe
when Svarang's sons assaulted me with stones!
They did not find the victory they sought,
for first they had to beg me for their lives!"

What were you doing in the meantime, Harbarð?"

Harbarð said:

30.   "In eastern lands I met a certain girl,
as white as linen, long I laid with her,
she shone like gold, we gave each other joy!"

Þor said:

31.   "Sounds like your journeys in the east went well!"

Harbarð said:

32.   "Back then I might have needed help from you,
so I could hold that beauty in my arms!"

Þor said:

33.   "If I had been there, I'd have gladly helped!"

Harbarð said:

34.   "I'd trust you then, if you did not betray me!"

Þor said:

35.   "I'm not a shriveled shoe; I bite no heels!"

Harbarð said:

36.   "What were you doing in the meantime, Þor?"

Þor said:

37.   "I went to Hlesey, fought berserkers' brides,
they were the worst, for they'd deceived mankind!"

Harbarð said:

38.   "What sort of man are you, who fights with girls?"

Þor said:

39.   "I'd hardly call them girls, but more like wolves!
        They smashed my ship when I'd just fixed it up,
        they chased Þjalfi,[35] threatened me with clubs!

        What were you doing in the meantime, Harbarð?"

Harbarð said:

40.   "I joined an army, and we passed this way
        we raised a flag, and stained our spears with blood!"

Þor said:

41.   "As I recall, you offered nasty threats!"

Harbarð said:

42.   "Then I will pay you back, I have a ring,
        I got it from a judge, for making peace!"

Þor said:

43.   "How did you come to know such vile words?
        In all my days I've never heard such filth!"[36]

Harbarð said:

44.   "The elders of my verdant home taught me!"

Þor said:

45.   "You flatter tombs, with names like 'verdant home'!"

Harbarð said:

46.   "That's how I like to think about these things!"

Þor said:

47.   "Your insolence won't help you worth a damn
        if I decide to wade across the fjord!
        I swear, you'll howl more loudly than a wolf
        when Mjolnir lands a single blow!"

---

[35] One of Þor's slaves.
[36] It's unclear why Þor is so offended by this statement.

Harbarð said:

48. "While you've been gone, your wife's been getting fucked,
if I were you, I'd save my strength for him!"

Þor said:

49. "Your tongue's as false as all the boasts you've made,
you gutless prick, I think you're full of shit!"

Harbarð said:

50. "I speak the truth, but Þor, you travel slow,
you'd travel far if you would move your ass!"

Þor said:

51. "You bitch, I think it's you who's slowed me down!"

Harbarð said:

52. "Who'd ever guess a simple shepherd could
so easily delay the mighty Þor!"

Þor said:

53. "We've fought enough, now row me over there,
for you'd do well to come meet Magni's dad!"

Harbarð said:

54. "I will do no such thing, now go away!"

Þor said:

55. "If that's the case, then tell me where to go!"

Harbarð said:

56. "It's easy to refuse, but hard to walk,
a mile to a stump, another to a stone,
and then go left until you get to Verland.
I know that Fjorgyn will be waiting there,
and she can ferry you to Oðin's land!"

Þor said:

57. "Will I be able to arrive today?"

Harbarð said:

58. "If you run hard and fast you should arrive
before the break of day, I'm pretty sure."

Þor said:

59. "I've nothing more to say, except for this:
I will repay the scorn you've shown in kind,
you'd better pray we never meet again."

Harbarð said:

60. "Fuck off! May fiends and devils eat you whole!"

Hymiskviða

How Þor Caught the Snake

Introduction

Hymiskviða "Hymir's Poem" is found both in the *Codex Regius* and the AM 748 I 4to, with the latter giving it its modern title; the *Regius* instead calls it *Þórr dró Miðgarðsormr* "Þor caught the Miðgarð-snake".

This poem begins a series that tell stories of the god Þor. It tells the tale of his quest for a cauldron large enough for the sea-devil Aegir to prepare the gods' feasts, leading to his titular encounter with Jormungand, the world-snake.

Hymiskviða is indisputably based on very old material. The motif of Þor fishing for Jormungand was very popular in Viking Age art, and can be seen on runestones from as far back as the 8th century. However, this version of the story shows signs of being a late creation, probably from the 11th or 12th centuries.

The poem makes extensive use of complex kennings, more so than any other Eddic poem, and sometimes uses strange word order, features both associated with the more complex meters employed by skalds. This suggests that the poem was composed by someone trained in skaldic verse, specifically the complex meters employed by court poets of around that time.

1.   In ancient days the gods had hunted game
and sought to hold a feast, and stuff themselves.
With twigs and blood they worked their augury
and found that Aegir's hall had many pots.

2.   There Aegir sat, as merry as a clam,[37]
when all the gods approached him in his hall.
Till Oðin's son declared, with flaming eyes,
"You'll host our feasts until the end of days!"

3.   When Aegir heard the gods' demands of him,
the fiend began to plot a cruel revenge.
He told the gods, "I'll need a certain pot,
a mile deep, so I can feed you all!"

4.   The blessed ones then scoured every world,
but could not find a pot so big as that
till loyal Tyr recalled a memory,
he went to Hlorriði,[38] and said to him,

5.   "My father, Hymir, lives in eastern lands
beyond the sky, beyond the ancient streams!
He's vicious, and his wisdom rivals none,
but I recall, he has the pot we need!"

6.   Þor asked, "Could we "acquire" it from him?"
Tyr said, "We could, if we combine our wits."

7.   And so they traveled far from Oðin's lands
beyond the rising sun, to Egil's house,
the man who tends the billy-goats for Þor;
and then from there they went to Hymir's hall.

8.   Tyr prayed his granny would not get the door,
he was repulsed by her nine hundred heads!
To his delight, his mother met them there,
she shone like gold, her brows were pearly white,
and as she poured the beer, she warned them thus:

---

[37] The manuscripts say "happy like Miskorblindi's son". Exactly what this refers to is unclear, so I have substituted an equivalent simile.
[38] "Roaring Rider", another name for Þor.

9.   "When Hymir comes, go hide beneath the pots,
        I'll see no harm upon my son and guest!
        My man is known to be a stingy host
        and everyone who knows him fears his wrath!"

10.   That twisted devil still had not returned,
        he'd gone out hunting and was coming late.
        But as she told them, Hymir came inside,
        his frozen beard was clanking as he walked.

11.   She called, "Hello, my husband, I have news,
        your son at last has come to visit us!
        He came from far away, and brought a friend,
        he came with foe of Hroð, the friend of man,
        the guardian of Earth, he's brought us Þor!

12.   They're in the gable, underneath the pots,
        behind a pillar, standing on the beam!"
        At Hymir's glance the pillar burst apart,
        the beam was split, and Tyr and Þor collapsed.

13.   Eight pots fell down, but one remained intact,
        a mile deep, and hammered hard as steel.
        They stood before their host, but Hymir's eyes
        were focused on the foe of every fiend.

14.   His heart was filled with evil when he saw
        the devils' widowmaker on the floor.
        He ordered that three bulls be brought inside
        and boiled, so his guests might have a meal.

15.   The bulls were shortened by their heads and horns
        and brought to boil in the cooking pit.
        Sif's man alone, before he went to sleep,
        had two of Hymir's oxen on his own!

16.   It seemed to Hrungnir's frosty friend[39] that Þor
        had eaten more than etiquette allowed.
        He said, "Tomorrow night we'll have to fish
        if we're to have a meal of equal size!"

17.   "I'll gladly row you out to sea," said Þor,
        "if you've got something I can use for bait!"
        "Alright, let's see if you are brave enough
        to fetch it from my herd, almighty Þor!"

18.   The breaker of the stony warriors
        should have no trouble with an ox's bits!"
        The son of Oðin went into the woods
        and there he found an ox as black as coal.

19.   He tore the horned meadow[40] off the bull,
        then god and devil braved the raging sea.
        Then Hymir said, "Your mighty deeds don't seem
        like much at all when you are sitting still!"

20.   Then Hymir, famous for his strength and rage,
        fished up a pair of whales all by himself,
        while at the stern the guardian of men
        was winding up a mighty fishing line.

21.   The lord of goats then asked the son of apes
        to row their mount as far as it would go.
        But Hymir said, "I fear that soon we'll reach
        the snake, and I've no urge to meet that beast."

22.   The thundering hero, born to kill the snake,
        then speared the ox's head upon the hook.
        The belt of Miðgarð gaped at such a snack,
        the bane of gods was pulled up from the depths.

---

[39] i.e., Hymir. "Hrungnir's friend" is a kenning for *devil*, with Hrungnir being a stone
devil that Þor once killed in a duel.
[40] Head.

23.   He dragged the Miðgarð serpent to the deck
and met the poisoned gaze of Jormungand.
He raised Mjolnir, and he slammed it down
upon the hairy hill of Fenrir's kin.

24.   Then monsters roared, the mountains all resounded,
the ancient earth was trembling at the deed,
and then the serpent sank beneath the waves.

25.   As Hymir rowed them back, his mood was grim,
until they reached the shore, his tongue was still,
and then he turned the rudder somewhere else,

26.   "Would you be kind enough to share the work
by taking both the whales back to the hall
or tying fast our floating steed to land?"

27.   Hlorriði rose, and grabbed it by the prow
alone he raised it up, with oars and bilge.
The whales were still aboard, he brought them too,
to Hymir's hall within the wooded gorge.

28.   And then the fiend, as stubborn as could be,
tried once again to find a match for Þor.
He said, "An average man can row a boat,
but no one's strong unless he breaks a cup."

29.   Hlorriði tried to smash the sturdy cup,
he flung it at the poles but split the stone!
At everything he saw he threw the glass,
but every time they brought it back intact.

30.   Till Hymir's wife spoke softly in his ear
and gave the thunder-maker good advice:
"The hardest thing in here is Hymir's head,
I know that it will smash the toughest glass!"

31.   The master of the billy-goats arose,
and mustered all the strength of godly blood!
There was no scratch on Hymir's helmet-stump,
but shards of glass were scattered on the floor.

32.   "It seems my finest treasure will depart,
since broken glass is scattered round my lap,"
the old man said. "I'll never say again,
'the ale is brewed, I've made enough for all!'

33.   The pot you've come to seek is over there,
let's see if you can get it out of here."
The first to try was Tyr, he did his best,
but twice the pot stood still before his might.

34.   Then Moði's father grabbed it by the rim
and pushed so hard his feet went through the floor.
Sif's husband raised the pot above his head,
the hanging-chains were clanking at his feet.

35.   The two had traveled far from Hymir's hall
when Oðin's son had made a stop to rest.
He turned and saw advancing from the east
a host of fiends, with Hymir at the head.

36.   He threw the hefty cauldron off his back
and raised his murder-happy hammer high,
then wiped that army from the face of earth.

37.   They had not traveled very far from there
before the goats of Þor were found half-dead.
Each one of them was lamed by evil spells,
a little courtesy from crafty Loki.

38.   But you all know, and everyone who's heard
the stories of the gods can tell the tale,
the payment he received for this offense:
the wild man gave Þor his kids as slaves.

39.   At last the mighty ones rejoined the gods,
and brought the pot, a mile deep, they sought.
And thus the holy ones could drink and feast
in Aegir's hall when winter[41] bore its teeth.

---

[41] Literally "poison-rope cutter". "Poison-ropes" are snakes, and their "cutter" must be winter, as the cold air kills snakes. This is an example of the complex kennings employed in skaldic poetry.

Lokasenna

Loki's Flyting

Introduction

Another of the Edda's most famous poems, *Lokasenna* "Loki's Dispute" is preserved only in the *Codex Regius*. It is among the most striking examples of flyting among the Eddic poems, both for its inclusion of many different opponents for Loki as well as for the vulgarity of many of the insults used (squeamish readers have been warned).

The poem deals entirely with its titular flyting, between Loki and all the other gods. Loki accuses the gods variously of dishonor, favoritism, and sexual impropriety, and though he wins the flyting, the gods respond by imprisoning him until Ragnarok.

There is solid linguistic evidence that *Lokasenna* predates the 11th century, in the form of several stanzas where the word *reið* "angry" alliterates with words beginning with *v*. This only makes sense if the poet pronounced *reið* as *vreið*, which is the older pronunciation of that word. Icelandic lost the initial *v* in the early 11th century, which means the poem must have been composed before then.

Aegir, who was also called Gymir, had prepared a great feast for the gods, after he received the mile-deep pot, as was told previously.

Oðin and his wife, Frigg, attended this feast. Þor could not make it, as he was away in the east, but his wife Sif was there, as were Bragi and his wife, Iðun. Tyr was there as well, and at this point had lost his right hand when the wolf was bound. Njorð attended too, as did his wife, Skaði, and his children, Frey and Freyja, as well as Frey's servants, Byggvir and Beyla, and Loki as well. Many other gods and elves attended as well.

Aegir had two servants, Fimafeng and Eldir. His hall was so decked out with gold that the sheen of the metal lit his hall instead of fire. It was a holy sanctuary, where the beer served itself. Aegir's servants were so good at their jobs that beings everywhere sang their praises for their dedication. Loki could not tolerate such praise, and so he murdered Fimafeng.

The gods rattled their shields and screamed at Loki, and chased him off into the woods, and then returned to their feasting and drinking. Loki turned back, and met Eldir outside the hall.

Loki greeted him thus:

1.   "Hello again, I'd like to know,
before you take another step;
what are the gods discussing there
that warrants such a gaudy feast?"

Eldir said:

2.   "The gods discuss their weapons, and
their battles and their bravery.
Among the gods and elves in there,
not one would dare call you a friend!"

Loki said:

3.   "I think I'll step inside the hall
and see this feast of noble gods!
I'll spread disgrace among the gods
and mix my poison in their mead!"

Eldir said:

4.   "Be warned: if you should step inside
and see the feast of noble gods,
and spread your slander on their names,
they'll surely throw it back at you!"

Loki said:

5.   "Keep talking shit, I'll gladly stay
and fight with you instead of them!
The more I hone my tongue on you,
the better I can shame the gods!"

Then Loki went into the hall, and the feast fell silent when everyone saw who had entered.

Loki said:

6.   "Hello, great gods, my name is Lopt,[42]
I'm parched, for I have traveled far
to ask the gods to share with me
a single sip of wondrous mead.

7.   Do all of you have heads so big
you won't address your latest guest?
Prepare for me a place to sit,
and if you won't, then chase me off!"

Bragi said:

8.   "No god would ever be so dumb
to set a seat aside for you!
The gods are wise enough to know
the types of beings we should host."

Loki said:

9.   "Have you forgotten, Oðin, that
in ancient days we mixed our blood?
We swore that we would never drink
if both of us could not get beer!"

---

[42] *air*, a poetic name for Loki.

Oðin said:

10. "Get up then, Viðar, clear your seat,
   the father of the wolf must sit.
   If not, then he'll speak vile words
   to us in Aegir's golden hall!"

Then Viðar got up, and poured Loki a drink. Before he drained it, he said:

11. "A toast to gods and goddesses,
   and everyone assembled here,
   except for Bragi over there,
   to him I say: Go fuck yourself!"

Bragi said:

12. "I'll give you treasures from my hoard:
   a horse, a sword, a golden ring,
   if that will let us feast in peace.
   Do not provoke the gods' revenge!"

Loki said:

13. "Since when do you possess a hoard
   of value that can end disputes?
   Of everyone assembled here,
   you have the greatest fear to fight
   and cannot shoot an arrow straight!"

Bragi said:

14. "You lying prick, if I were not
   a guest in Aegir's golden hall,
   I'd mount your head upon a spike
   and still that wouldn't sate my rage!"

Loki said:

15. "Your words are brave, but not your deeds,
   Bragi, Keeper of the Bench!
   If you're so angry, let's step out,
   the valiant never fear to fight!"

Iðun said:

16. "My husband, please don't run your mouth,
for you dishonor Aegir's hall.
Though Loki's crude, he's still our kin,
adoption binds as strong as blood!"

Loki said:

17. "Yes, tell me all the things you know
about the bonds of family!
You fucked your brother's killer, bitch,
I've never seen such lust for dick!"

Iðun said:

18. "I won't repay your words in kind
while we are guests in Aegir's hall!
My man is drunk, I'll keep him calm,
I don't want fights to wreck the feast!"

Gefjun said:

19. "Why must we clash with wounding words
when we have feasting to enjoy?
We all know Lopt's a goofy guy
and that's why he is much beloved."

Loki said:

20. "Now shut your mouth, you vapid slut
whose cunt is also much beloved!
A necklace was enough for you
to give away your maidenhood!"

Oðin said:

21. "My friend, you've truly lost your mind
if you would rouse the rage of Gefjun!
She knows the fates of gods and elves
at least as well as me, I think!"

Loki said:

22. "Be quiet, Oðin, for you can't
give victory to worthy men!
You've let too many cowards win
in battle when the valiant should!"

Oðin said:

23. "My judgments are not always right,
some weak men gain the victory,
but eight long years you spent on earth
in woman's shape; you milked their cows
and fucked their men, and had their kids,
so you will always be a bitch!"

Loki said:

24. "Quite rich from you, did you not go
to Samsey, wearing witches' clothes?[43]
I know men saw you dressed like that,
so you're the greatest bitch of all!"

Frigg said:

25. "It's never wise to speak aloud
of shame that fate has brought on you!
Forget the things you did back then,
let what has passed stay in the past!"

Loki said:

26. "Be quiet, Frigg, you're Fjorgyn's girl,
and have her beat in thirst for men!
The moment Oðin left, you had
both Ve and Vili in your bed!"

Frigg said:

27. "If Baldr still was at my side,
he'd raise his blade in my defense
and you would not escape from him
till he repaid your lies in blood!"

Loki said:

28. "I wonder why your precious boy
will never greet you in your hall?
It's almost like I got him killed
and now you must defend yourself!"

---

[43] Cross-dressing was a severe taboo in Norse society, as was the use of magic by men.

Freyja said:

29.   "I think you've truly lost your mind
to speak such vile words to Frigg!
We both know Frigg knows every fate,
although she keeps it to herself!"

Loki said:

30.   "Be quiet, whore, I know you well,
you only think of getting fucked!
Each god and elf within this hall
has given you their dick for free!"

Freyja said:

31.   "You can't control your lying tongue,
and it's not serving you too well!
You've drawn the wrath of all the gods,
we'll make your life a living hell!"

Loki said:

32.   "I said shut up, you vile witch!
Your mind is so degenerate,
we found you once in Frey's embrace,
and then you loosed a mighty fart!"

Njorð said:

33.   "There is no shame if women have
a lover and a husband, too,
besides, you've had it up the ass
and even given birth, you bitch!"

Loki said:

34.   "Now shut your mouth and keep it shut,
you're but a hostage, not a god!
You're just the devils' urinal,
they're always pissing in your mouth!"

Njorð said:

35.   "There is one thing that's brought me pride
and joy while I've been far from home:
I raised a son who no one hates,
and he's the highest of the gods!"

Loki said:

36.   "Don't run your mouth if that's your best,
for I know something no one does:
Your sister birthed your precious boy,
and I'd expect no more from you!"

Tyr said:

37.   "It's widely known that Frey's the best
and bravest rider of the gods,
he's never harmed a girl or wife,
and always frees the wrongly chained!"

Loki said:

38.   "Be quiet, Tyr! You never could
resolve disputes in helpful ways!
Besides, you've got a ragged stump
where Fenrir tore your hand away!"

Tyr said:

39.   "I lack a hand, you lack your son,
I think your pain is more than mine!
Your precious whelp must wait in chains
until the doom of gods arrives!"

Loki said:

40.   "Be quiet, Tyr! You have no son,
the boy you've raised in fact is mine!
I'll pay no pennies for your pain
nor half a yard of cloth,[44] you cuck!"

Frey said:

41.   "Your boy is bound, and forms a stream
until the gods are ripped apart,
you'll think his life luxurious
if you don't shut your mouth and leave!"

---

[44] Originally measured from the fingertips to the elbow. Since Tyr is missing a forearm, "an arm of cloth" could be a veiled insult.

Loki said:

42.   "You could not buy your wife with gold,
instead, you gave your sword away,
and so, when Muspell's fire comes,
you'll die in searing pain, alone!"

Byggvir said:

43.   "If I had blood like Ingun-Frey[45]
and sat in such a lofty seat,
I'd grind your bones and shred your limbs,
and turn you into bloody bread!"

Loki said:

44.   "What tiny thing is barking now
and thinks I fear its wagging tail?
It's always perched atop Frey's ear
and sings its songs upon his mills!"

Byggvir said:

45.   "My name is Byggvir, every god
and man knows my agility!
It brings me joy that sons of Hropt
can gather here and drink in peace!"

Loki said:

46.   "Be quiet, then, you drunken dick,
you cannot fairly feed mankind!
You can't be found among the straw
when men decide it's time to fight!"

Heimdall said:

47.   "You've lost your mind, you're deadly drunk,
why can't you keep your tongue contained?
When morning comes, you will regret
the stupid things you've said tonight."

---

[45] Ingun, or Yngvi in other sources, is the Norse descendant of *Ingwaz*, the name of an ancient Germanic deity whio may or may not be the same as Frey.

Loki said:

48.   "Be quiet, Heimdall, for your life
is always filled with misery!
With rigid back you always stand
and, never sleeping, guard the gods!"

Skaði said:

49.   "You think you're being cute, but you
will soon regret your rambling tongue!
We'll shred your son, and use his guts
to bind you to a freezing edge!"

Loki said:

50.   "If you're so fragile, go ahead
and bind me to a freezing edge!
I was the first to come and last
to go the day that Þjazi died!"

Skaði said:

51.   "If that's the case, that you were first
and last the day my father died,
then in my lands will always get
a frigid greeting when you come!"

Loki said:

52.   "Your words are harsh, but I must say,
if we're recounting our mistakes,
Your words to me were soft and sweet
when you were begging for my dick!"

Then Sif got up and gave Loki a frosted cup full of mead, and said:

53.   "I greet you, Loki, and I have
for you a glass of wondrous mead!
You may speak ill of other gods,
but know that I am free from faults!"

He took a horn, drained it, and said:

54.   "You'd live alone if you indeed
avoided men, as rumor says!
But there is one you do not shun,
besides the one you're married to,
who fucks you good when Þor is gone,
and that, as you're aware, is me!"

Beyla said:

55.   "The mountains tremble, sky resounds,
I think that Þor is on his way!
He'll make you shut your lying mouth
and shield the names of gods and men!"

Loki said:

56.   "Be quiet, girl, you're Byggvir's wife
and thus, you have no right to judge!
There is no fouler being here,
you're filthy, and you smell like shit!"

Then Þor arrived, and said:

57.   "Be quiet, coward, or I will
deprive you of your lying tongue!
I'll split your neck and shoulder-hill
and take your useless life away!"

Loki said:

58.   "Hello there, Þor, and welcome back!
Why must you speak such nasty words?
I know you will not be so brave
when Fenrir swallows Oðin whole!"

Þor said:

59.   "Be quiet, coward, or I will
deprive you of your lying tongue!
I'll launch your head to Jotunheim,
and they won't find a scrap of you!"

Loki said:

60.   "I would not speak of Jotunheim
        if I were you, now, son of Earth!
        I watched you cower in a thumb,
        in fear you hid inside a glove,
        and then you hardly seemed like Þor!"

Þor said:

61.   "Be quiet, coward or I will
        deprive you of your lying tongue!
        I'll smash your bones with Hrungnir's bane
        and grind your flesh into a pulp!"

Loki said:

62.   "I aim to live a while yet,
        and though I fear your hammer's strike,
        I must remind you that the straps
        of Skrymir[46] were too much for you,
        and then you nearly starved to death!"

Þor said:

63.   "Be quiet, coward, or I will
        deprive you of your lying tongue!
        I'll knock your lying ass to hell,
        beyond the gates where corpses lie!"

Loki said:

64.   "I've said the things I want to say
        in Aegir's hall, before the gods.
        For you alone I will depart,
        because I know your threats are true!

65.   Your beer's delightful, Aegir, but
        you'll never make a feast again!
        May flames consume the things you own
        and scald your back as well!"

---

[46] A reference another part of the same tale of Skrymir mentioned in *Hárbarðsljóð*, where Þor fails to open Skrymir's bag, which is bound with magic wire.

After his departure, Loki disguised himself as a salmon and hid in the Sparkling Falls. There the gods caught him. He was tied up with the guts of Nari, his son. But Narfi, his son, turned into a wolf. Skaði took a venomous snake and tied it up above Loki's face, so that its poison dripped into his eyes. Loki's wife, Sigyn, sat there and held a bowl up to catch the venom. But when this bowl filled, she had to turn away to drain it, and the poison would fall onto his face. The pain made him writhe so violently that it shook the entire earth, and humans know these tremors as earthquakes.

Þrymskviða

How Þor Lost his Hammer

Introduction

Þrymskviða "Þrym's Poem" is preserved only in the *Codex Regius*, though its basic story survived for centuries in the form of folk ballads, preserved in the 19th century.

The poem's plot follows the theft of Þor's hammer, Mjolnir, and the gods' attempt to reclaim it by forcing Þor to disguise himself in a bridal gown, a comedic inversion of his usual hyper-masculinity.

The date of composition has proven among the most controversial of the eddic poems. Advocates for an early date point to the first line, which may contain a case of *reið* alliterating with *v*, and to the extensive use of the filler word *um*, which often occurs before verbs that in early Norse would have had a prefix *ga*, indicating completion association, and for forming participles of verbs. However, advocates of a late date point to the complete lack of references to its events anywhere else, neither in the *Prose Edda* or in any skaldic kennings. As with some other poems, it may be that this is a later composition based on earlier material, or perhaps it is an older poem that only reached Iceland at a late date, which might explain both its archaisms and the lack of references in earlier literature.

1.   One morning Þor awoke enraged
        and missed his hammer's grip.
        His hair and beard were flailing hard
        throughout his fumbling search.

2.   He said to Loki first of all,
        "I have to speak to you!
        Not once on earth or heaven's heights
        have things like this occurred!
        My hammer's gone, and can't be found,
        we need to find the thief!"

3.   They went to lovely Freyja's lands,
        and promptly Þor declared,
        "I need to take your feather-cloak
        so Mjolnir can be found."

4.   She said, "I'd let you have it if
        it was the finest thing I owned!"

5.   Then Loki flew, with rustling wings,
        beyond the realm of gods
        until at last he traveled to
        the lands of Jotunheim.

6.   There on a barrow he found Þrym,
        the lord and liege of fiends.
        He wove gold bands for all his dogs
        and trimmed his horses' manes.

7.   "What's brought you out to Jotunheim?
        How are the gods and elves?"
        "The gods and elves are trembling,
        is Mjolnir hidden here?"

8.   "I sealed it deep within the earth,
        you'll never get it back
        unless I get a good reward:
        sweet Freyja as my wife!"

9.   Then Loki flew, with rustling wings,
        away from Jotunheim
        until at last he traveled to
        the realm of gods again.
        There Þor was waiting at the gates,
        and, lacking patience, yelled,

10.   "What news have you from Jotunheim?
        Tell me before you land!
        For sitting men have slippery minds,
        and liars earn no faith!"

11.   "I've found your hammer, and a mess!
        The thief was Þrym, and he
        will only give it back if we
        make Freyja marry him!"

12.   They went to lovely Freyja's lands
        and told her Þrym's demands.
        "Put on your bridal gown," they said,
        "we're off to Jotunheim!"

13.   But Freyja's fury shook the Earth,
        her blazing necklace cracked!
        She yelled, "I'm hardly such a slut
        to sleep in devils' beds!"

14.   The gods then gathered in a rush
        and goddesses as well,
        they sat there long, and long they schemed
        to get Mjolnir back.

15.   Then shining Heimdall hatched a plan,
        for he knew fate like Vanir.
        "Have Þor go there in Freyja's dress,
        and wear her flaming clasp!

16.   We'll dangle keys upon his belt,
        and skirts around his legs,
        we'll put her jewels upon his chest,
        and tie his hair in braids!"

17.   "The gods will think that I'm a bitch
         if I do such a thing!
         I'd sooner never fight again
         than wear a linen gown."

18.   "Be quiet, Þor, and suck it up,"
         said Loki Laufey's son,
         "The devils will destroy us all
         if you don't don the veil."

19.   So Þor was bound in bridal wear
         and Freyja's shining chain,
         her keys were hung upon his belt,
         and skirts around his knees,
         her jewels were glinting on his chest,
         his hair was bound in braids!

20.   "I'll be your maid of honor, Þor,"
         said Loki, Laufey's son,
         "I'll go with you to Jotunheim,
         for this I have to see!"

21.   And so the goats were driven hard,
         their halters nearly broke,
         the mountains split, and Earth was scorched
         as Oðin's son rode off!

22.   When they arrived, lord Þrym declared,
         "Arise and set the seats!
         For Freyja's here to marry me,
         my prize from Noatun!"

23.   My lands are filled with golden cows
         and oxen black as coal,
         I have a hoard of gold and gems,
         it's only her I lack!"

24.   When they arrived, at sun's descent,
         the beer was poured for them.
         "She" ate an ox, and many fish,
         and all the women's snacks;
         "she" drank three kegs of mead as well,

and drank his barrels dry!

25.   The lord of fiends was quite confused,
        and he declared, in shock,
        "Whoever saw a woman eat
        with vigor such as that?
        Or drink three kegs of mead alone
        until my stores are gone?'

26.   "Her" clever bridesmaid, in the front,
        responded fast as light,
        "Eight days and nights she starved herself,
        she was so hyped to come!"

27.   He craved "her" lips, and raised "her" veil,
        but then leapt back in fright.
        "I've never seen such frightful eyes,
        they burn like blazing suns!'

28.   "Her" clever bridesmaid, in the front,
        responded fast as light,
        "Eight days and nights she stayed awake,
        she was so hyped to come!"

29.   Þrym's sister came into the hall
        to seek the bridal fee.
        "Now give me, girl, your golden rings,
        if you would win my love!"

30.   Then Þrym announced, his patience thin,
        "Now bring Mjolnir in
        and place it in her lap; may Var
        our union consecrate!"

31.   Hlorriði burst with joy and cheer
        to feel his hammer's grip!
        He slaughtered Þrym, the lord of fiends,
        and all his family.

32.   His sister got a poor reward
        for all her great demands!
        She got concussed instead of coin,
        and death in place of rings!

And that's how Mjolnir was returned to Oðin's son.

Alvissmál

The Deception of Alviss

Introduction

Alvissmál "The Words of All-Wise" is preserved only in the *Codex Regius*. It is both the final encyclopedic poem of the Edda, as well as the finale of its series of poems focusing on Þor.

Unlike the other encyclopedic poems, which chronicle cosmological information, *Alvissmál* is instead a dictionary of poetic terms used for various objects in the natural world. Its frame plot revolves around Þor's attempts to barter with the titular dwarf Alviss, who seeks to marry the god's daughter.

Also unlike the other encyclopedic poems, whose nature makes them likely pre-Christian, *Alvissmál*'s role as a poetic dictionary does not rule out a later date of composition. A post-Christian date would explain a few references to beings called *uppregin* "high powers", distinct from the Norse gods. These might be angels or other Christian entities, which would suggest a date in perhaps the 11th or 12th centuries.

1.   "At last a bride shall decorate my home,
a lovely lady shall be seen with me!
The dwarves will think we fell in love at once
at home I'll see to it she gets no rest!"

2.   "What are you, friend? You're pale as death!
Have you been cuddling with a corpse?
You seem to me like kin of fiends,
I do not think you're fit for brides!"

3.   "My name is Alviss, from beneath the earth,
I have a manor underneath the stones.
I've traveled far to see the wagon man,[47]
I know his promises are always true!"

4.   "I'm here to break them, for I am
the one who has control of her!
Her hand was pledged while I was gone,
but she is mine to give away."

5.   "That girl's as lovely as the rising sun,
and I'm supposed to think she's kin of yours?
You filthy peasant, none will think she's yours!
Who really owns those golden rings you wear?"

6.   "My name is Þor, I've traveled far,
I am the son of Siðgrani!
You will not have my daughter's hand
if you cannot win my consent."

7.   "Then here and now I will win your consent,
I yearn the most to be a married man.
I'd rather have than live a day without
that beauty, white as flour, in my arms."

8.   "And you will have her in your arms
and then return beneath the earth,
if you can answer what I ask:
I seek the wisdom of the worlds.

---

[47] Probably Oðin, who is elsewhere called *vagns vinr* "friend of wagons" and *Farmatýr* "Cargo-God".

9.   Now, Alviss, tell me this, if you
        indeed are wisest of the dwarves,
        the earth which looms before mankind,
        what is it called in every world?"

10.   "It's known as Earth to men, and Field to gods,
        the fiends have named it Evergreen, the elves
        call it the Grower, Vanir call it Road,
        and all the higher ones have named it Mud."

11.   "Now, Alviss, tell me this, if you
        indeed are wisest of the dwarves,
        the sky that's known to holy ones,
        what is it called in every world?"

12.   "It's Heaven to mankind, but Lights to gods,
        the Vanir call it Weaver of the Winds,
        to fiends it's Upper World, Lovely Roof to elves,
        among the dwarves it's called the Dripping Hall."

13.   "Now, Alviss, tell me this, if you
        indeed are wisest of the dwarves,
        the moon that men can always see,
        what is it called in every world?"

14.   "It's Moon to men, but Crescent to the gods,
        in Niflheim it's called the Whirling Wheel,
        it's Dasher to the fiends, but Shine to dwarves,
        the elves have named it Counter of the Years."

15.   "Now, Alviss, tell me this, if you
        indeed are wisest of the dwarves,
        the sun, which always lights the earth,
        what is it called in every world?

16.   "Among both men and gods it's called the Sun,
        the dwarves refer to it as Dvalin's toy,
        it's Lovely Wheel to elves, and Ever-Bright
        to fiends, and All-Bright to the sons of gods."

17.   "Now, Alviss, tell me this, if you
        indeed are wisest of the dwarves,
        the clouds which mix with ice and rain,
        what are they called in every world?"

18.   "They're Clouds to men, but Vanir call them Floats,
        among the gods they're Bringers of the Rain,
        the dead know them as Hiding Helms, the elves
        the Strength of Storms, and fiends the Drizzlers."

19.   "Now, Alviss, tell me this, if you
        indeed are wisest of the dwarves,
        the wind which travels far and wide,
        what is it called in every world?"

20.   "It's Wind to men, but Roamer to the gods,
        Noise-Goer to the elves, and Howler to
        the fiends, but Brayer to the holy ones,
        it's called the Squaller in the halls of Hel."

21.   "Now, Alviss, tell me this, if you
        indeed are wisest of the dwarves,
        the calm that comes when all is still,
        what is it called in every world?"

22.   "It's Calm to men, but Stillness to the gods,
        The Vanir call it Silence of the Wind,
        to dwarves it's Shield of Day, to fiends it's called
        the Sultry One, and Soother to the elves."

23.   "Now, Alviss, tell me this, if you
        indeed are wisest of the dwarves,
        the sea which sailors row upon,
        what is it called in every world?"

24.   "It's Sea to men, to gods it's Ever-Still,
        it's Surge to Vanir, Depths to dwarvenkind,
        the fiends all know it as the House of Eels,
        while elvenkind has named it Staff of Waves."

25. “Now, Alviss, tell me this, if you
indeed are wisest of the dwarves,
the flame that burns before mankind,
what is it called in every world?”

26. “It’s Flame to men, but Fire to the gods,
it’s Surge to Vanir, Scorcher to the dwarves,
the fiends all know it as the Greedy One,
the guests of Hel have named it Hurrier.”

27. “Now, Alviss, tell me this, if you
indeed are wisest of the dwarves,
the wood that comes from fallen trees,
what is it called in every world?”

28. “It’s Wood to men, but Hair of Fields to gods,
in Niflheim it’s Seaweed of the Hills,
it’s Lovely-Limbed to elves, and Fire-Wood
to all the fiends, while Vanir call it Wand.”

29. “Now, Alviss, tell me this, if you
indeed are wisest of the dwarves,
the night, the starry girl of Norr,
what is she called in every world?”

30. “She’s Night to men, but Darkness to the gods
as well as Mask, to elves she’s Joy of Sleep,
the fiendish ones have named her Lack of Light,
She’s Lady of the Dreams to dwarvenkind.”

31. “Now, Alviss, tell me this, if you
indeed are wisest of the dwarves,
the seeds that feed the sons of men,
what are they called in every world?”

32. “They’re Seeds to men, but Barley to the gods,
the Vanir call them Growth, to fiends it’s Food,
for elves, they are the Drinking Staves, the dead
in Niflheim call them the Dangling Plants.

33. "Now, Alviss, tell me this, if you
    indeed are wisest of the dwarves,
    the ale that humans love to drink,
    what is it called in every world?"

34. "It's Ale to men, but Beer among the gods,
    in Niflheim it's Mead, to Suttung's sons
    its names are Drink and Shining Liquid, and
    it's Liquor to the sons of Vanaheim."

35. "In all my years I've never seen
    such knowledge in a single mind!
    Alas, it seems you're not so wise,
    for all your smarts, you've still been duped!
    The sun is up, and so are you,
    the dawn will be your final sight!"[48]

---

[48] It has long been believed that the sun turns Alviss to stone here, though the text never explicitly states that.

Skírnismál

Skirnir's Travels

Introduction

This poem is preserved in the *Codex Regius*, where it is titled *Fǫr Skírnis* "Skirnir's Journey" (the source of its English name in this book) and its first 27 stanzas are also found in the AM 748 I 4to manuscript, from which it gets its usual modern title *Skírnismál* "Skirnir's Words". In the *Regius*, it is found after *Grímnismál*, but I have moved it here to keep the Oðin- and Þor-poems together.

This is the only Eddic poem to focus on the god Frey as a major character. The poem tells of how he fell in love with Gerð, the devil woman who would become his wife, and of his manservant Skirnir's attempts to persuade her to marry Frey.

Nothing about *Skírnismál* suggests a particularly early or late date, and its age has been much disputed. Its lack of obvious Christian influence might suggest an early date, while advocates of a late date point to a resemblance between Frey's longing for Gerð and the courtly love of medieval romance. However, stories of the gods were still told after the conversion, and love-sickness is not a concept unique to high medieval Europe. Dates between the 9th and 13th century have all been suggested, but none have been convincingly proven.

Frey, son of Njorð, was sitting in Hliðskjalf one day, looking across all the worlds. He looked into Jotunheim, and there he saw a beautiful woman walking to her chambers from her father's hall. Upon seeing her, Frey was stricken with desire, and he was wracked with awful sickness of the heart. Njorð asked Frey's servant, Skirnir, to find out what was wrong with his son.

Then Skaði said:

1. "Arise, my servant Skirnir, and go ask
my son the reason why his heart is ill!
Go make him tell you who has drawn his wrath
and what they did to make his wisdom fade!"

Skirnir said:

2. "Accursed words are all I'll get from him
if I approach my lord and try to find
the reason why his heart has fallen ill,
or what occurred to make his anger wax."

3. "My friend and lord, commander of the gods,
I fear for you, and so I want to know,
why do you waste away inside your hall
alone, avoiding light of sun, for days?"

Frey said:

4. "Why should I share my heart with you, old friend?
It will not end the great despair I feel!
I sulk because the elven beams[49] are bright,
but cannot pierce the gloom that shrouds my heart."

Skirnir said:

5. "You have no burdens too extreme to share,
for I will help in any way I can!
We've known each other since our swaddling days,
you know you always can rely on me."

---

[49] Sunbeams. The Norse associated elves with sunlight.

Frey said:

6.   "In Jotunheim I saw a gorgeous girl,
her name is Gerð, she's Gymir's daughter, and
her shining beauty lights the sky and sea,
forevermore I want her at my side."

7.   "I need her more than I need anything,
in all my years I've never wanted more!
But all the gods and elves will disapprove
if I should seek to claim her as my bride."

Skirnir said:

8.   "Then loan to me your horse that rides across
the famous flames that veil the devils' lands,
and give to me your sword which fights alone
against the clan of devils and their host."

Frey said:

9.   "I'll lend to you my horse that rides across
the famous flames that veil the devils' lands,
and give to you my sword which fights alone
if it is wielded by a worthy man."

Then Skirnir said to the horse:

10.   "The sun has set, I think it is the perfect time
to travel far across the rainy peaks
and gallop hard across the devils' lands!
We have a task to do, and if we fail,
then Gymir surely will consume us whole!"

Skirnir rode to Jotunheim, and then to Gymir's lands. He reached Gerð's hall, but found it surrounded by a vast fence and guarded by vicious dogs. He found a shepherd sitting on a barrow, and said to him:

11.   "Hey, you, the one who's lazing on the mound
and staring at the road, I'd like to know,
is there a way to get past Gymir's dogs
and see the girl who lives within his hall?"

12.   "Are you insane or suicidal, friend?
        In all of Jotunheim there are no halls
        as tightly kept as his; you'll never get
        to see that lovely girl, or speak to her!"

                    Skirnir said:
13.   "There's better things to do than sit and cry
        for those of us who walk the path of life!
        When I was born, my fate was put in place
        and on that day my life and deeds were set!"

                     Gerð said:
14.   "What is that awful noise I hear outside
        which loudly echoes through my father's halls?
        The earth is trembling, and my father's lands
        are being shaken to the very core!"

                 A serving-girl said:
15.   "A man's outside, he's just got off his horse
        and left it in your father's fields to graze."

                     Gerð said:
16.   "Then welcome him into my father's hall
        and pour for him a glass of glory-mead,
        Although I fear that standing at the door
        is someone who will prove my enemy."

17.   "Who are you, friend? Are you an elf, perhaps,
        or Vanir, or are you of godly blood?
        What's brought you by yourself across the flame
        and past the hounds, to visit Gymir's hall?"

                    Skirnir said:
18.   "I am no elf, I'm certainly no god,
        indeed I'm not a man of Vanaheim.
        I've come alone across the mighty flame
        to talk to you, and offer you a prize."

19.   "I've brought eleven golden apples here,
        a gift for you, to earn my lord your love.
        You'll get them if you pledge yourself to Frey
        and say that he's the greatest man of all!"

Gerð said:

20.   "Eleven golden apples aren't enough
to make me bow before a man's desire!
I will not live with Frey, nor share a bed
with him, as long as I can still draw breath!"

Skirnir said:

21.   "I've brought a golden ring for you as well,
that burned with Oðin's boy, and came from Hel.
Each ninth night, it will spawn eight copies of
itself; with it you'll never want for wealth!"

Gerð said:

22.   "I'll take no ring from you, especially
the one that burned with Oðin's little boy!
My father has no lack of gold or jewels,
I have no need to take another's wealth!"

Skirnir said:

23.   "Do you not see the rippling, gleaming blade
that rests upon my side, you stupid girl?
I swear I'll cleave your head and neck apart
if you won't marry who I tell you to!"

Gerð said:

24.   "I will not bow my head to idle threats
or serve a man who thinks with just his sword!
But I believe if Gymir finds you here
he will not fear to face that blade of yours!"

Skirnir said:

25.   "Do you not see the devil-slaying blade
that rests upon my side, you stupid girl?
Your father's weak, he cannot face my blade,
for fate's declared that it will end his life!

26.   Before I came, I went into the woods
to find a sappy tree, and make a wand,
and found the perfect tree to make a wand.

27.   I'll strike you with my magic wand, you brat,
       I swear, you'll do the things I tell you to,
       or else I'll send you where no living things
       will ever see, or think of, you again!

28.   Upon the eagles' hill you'll pine away
       and beg to be a guest in Hel's estate,
       The sight of food will make your stomach lurch
       as humans' do when they lay eyes on snakes!

29.   And when you step outside, you'll be a sight!
       For every man alive will gawk at you
       as Heimdall stares at worlds; your fame will match
       his own, and in your prison you shall weep!

30.   Your life will fill with rage and endless pain,
       you'll always scream with never-ending lust!
       I'm hardly done, for now I'll tell you of
       the sea of sorrow, torment, constant grief
       that you shall face for all your useless days!

31.   You'll be the favorite toy of Jotunheim
       and pass the days enslaved in devils' lands!
       To frosty halls you'll have to go each day
       without a choice, by someone else's will!
       You'll pleasure them, and never cease to cry,
       your tears will ever wet your sorrow-fields.

32.   A monster with three heads will be your man,
       or else you'll live your life without a man!
       You'll yearn for dick, but not be satisfied,
       your lust will fill you up until you burst
       like thistle-flowers when the harvest comes!

33.   You'll earn the wrath of Oðin and of Þor,
       forevermore you'll have the hate of Frey,
       you vile bitch, the only thing you'll have
       is mighty rage, from every single god!

34.   Now hear me, devils, hear me, frosty ones,
      and hear me, sons of Suttung, and the gods!
      For now I ban, forever I forbid
      that men should greet this girl with friendly words
      and I forbid that they should pleasure her!

35.   I'll give you to the fiendish Hrimgrimnir,
      he'll have you down below the gates of death!
      And when you reach the roots of Yggdrasil
      you'll only have the piss of goats to drink!
      You'll swear you've never had a better drink,
      for that will be my wish as well as yours!

36.   Now Þ[50] I'll carve for you, as well as spells,
      perversion, frenzy, and eternal lust!
      I will remove the runes I've carved for you,
      if you will give me cause to set you free!"

Gerð said:

37.   "Then hail, my friend, and have a glass of mead
      and have it in my finest frosted cup.
      In all my years, I'd never have believed
      that I would have a Vanir for a man!"

Skirnir said:

38.   "There's one more thing I need to hear from you
      before I tell my lord that he's engaged:
      I need to know the day you'll give yourself
      in marriage to the virile son of Njorð."

Gerð said:

39.   "There is a place called Barri he should know,
      a sacred grove where air is ever still,
      in nine nights' time, I'll meet the son of Njorð
      and he will have a night he won't forget."

---

[50] Called *þurs*, "fiend", this rune was associated with harm to women.

Then Skirnir rode home. Frey was waiting for him, and anxiously asked:

40.   "Hail, my friend, before you leave the horse
        or take another step, I want to know:
        What happened when you went to Jotunheim?
        Did you fulfill my greatest wish, or yours?"

Skirnir said:
41.   "There is a grove called Barri, you should know,
        she said she'll meet you there in nine nights' time.
        She said you'll have a night you won't forget-
        you have your prize, now saddle up and go!"

Frey said:
42.   "A night is long, a second longer still,
        I do not know if I can wait for three.
        It feels to me a month is shorter than
        just half a night of longing for my love!"

Hyndluljóð

Hyndla's Prophecy

Introduction

Hyndluljóð "Hyndla's Song" is preserved only in the 14th-century manuscript *Flateyarbók*. It is also quoted in the *Prose Edda*, though Snorri attributes the quoted verse to a poem titled *Vøluspá hin skamma* "The Little Vøluspá". This has caused much scholarly hand-wringing over whether *Hyndluljóð* and *Vøluspá hin skamma* are in fact the same poem, and if not, how much of the latter was incorporated into the former. The simplest explanation, however, is that the two are the same poem, known by different names in different places and times. The text flows fine as written, and shows no signs of additions.

This is the only Eddic poem to prominently feature the goddess Freyja as a major character. It follows her efforts to aid a mortal lover of hers, Ottar, by recruiting a devil woman named Hyndla to inform him of his prestigious heritage.

Hyndluljóð is almost certainly a late poem. Its other title means it must have been composed after *Vøluspá*, and one of its stanzas likely contains a vague reference to Jesus. It is no older than the 11th century, and is likely to be younger than that.

Here begins Hyndla's Song, told about Ottar the Stupid.

Freyja said:

1.   "Wake up, my girl! Wake up, my friend,
my sister,[51] Hyndla, in the cave!
The mighty twilight's come, let's ride
to Valhall and the holy shrine!

2.   Let's ask for Herjafoðr's help,
for he gives gold to those who've earned it!
From him came Hermoð's helm and mail
and Sigmund's blade that he received.

3.   He gives out victory and wealth,
and eloquence and wisdom, too,
to sailors wind, to poets words,
and bravery to warriors.

4.   I'll offer blood to Þor, and ask
that he be always kind to you,
though he does not like devils' wives!

5.   Now lead a wolf out from its stall
and let it run beside my boar!"

Hyndla said:

6.   "Your barrow's slow to walk the godly road!
Besides, I won't wear down my finest steed!

7.   You're devious, miss Freyja, when you look
at us like that, and when you test me so!
You've brought your lover as a boar,
for I can see that's Ottar, Innstein's son!"

---

[51] Freyja and Hyndla are not siblings. Freyja is either being sarcastic or buttering Hyndla up.

136

Freyja said:

8. "You're crazy, Hyndla, if you think
   I've brought my man on deadly roads!
   I have my golden-bristled boar,
   his name is Hildisvin, and he
   was made by dwarves named Dain and Nabbi.

9. Now let's dismount, and settle down,
   and then discuss the kin of boars[52]
   and men who bear the blood of gods.

10. With foreign gold a bet was made
    by Ottar and by Angantyr.
    I seek to help, so he may gain
    inheritance of Innstein's lands.

11. He made an altar, stacked with stones,
    its flames have turned the rocks to glass.
    He stained it red with blood of bulls,
    for Ottar's true to goddesses.

12. Now tell me all the ancient names
    of those who long ago were born
    of Skjoldung's sons and Skilfing's kin,
    of Auðling's blood and Ylfing's clan,
    those born of freemen and of kings,
    the greatest choice of Miðgarð's sons!"

Hyndla said:

13. "Now Ottar, as I said, is Innstein's son,
    and Innstein's father's name was Alf the Old,
    and Alf's was Ulf, and Ulf's was Saevari,
    and Saevari was born to Svan the Red.

14. Your father's mother was quite flush with wealth,
    I think she was a priestess known as Hledis,
    Her mother's name was Flaut, her father's Froði,
    her kin are known to be the greatest men.

---

[52] There is an untranslatable pun here; *boar* is a common poetic word for *prince*. Freyja admits her boar is, in fact, Ottar, by asking for information about his kin.

15.   Before that, Ali was the greatest man
and Halfdan, highest of the Skjoldung clan,
he fought in battles famous far and wide,
his deeds were known to those at heaven's end.

16.   By marriage he was one of Eymund's kin,
and slaughtered Sigtrygg with a frozen blade.
He married Almveig, greatest wife there was,
she bore him eighteen sons, and raised them well.

17.   The Skjoldungs and the Skilfings came from them,
as did the Auðlings and the Ynglings, too,
from them came sons of freemen and of kings,
the greatest choice of Miðgarð's residents,
and that's your family, Ottar, stupid boy!

18.   Now Almveig's mother's name was Hildigunn,
the girl of Svava and of Saekonung,
they're all your family, Ottar, stupid boy,
and you should know it, too; shall I go on?

19.   Then Dag, the son of Halfdan, married Þora,
who's called the Heroes' Mother, for she birthed
Gyrð and Fraðmar and the two named Freki,
and Am and Josurmar and Alf the Old,
these names are good to know; shall I go on?

20.   They had a friend named Ketill, son of Klypp,
he was your mother's father's father, boy,
he fathered Froði first, and Kari next,
and then the elder Alf was born the third.

21.   Then next is Nanna, Nokkvi's girl,
your in-law's father had a son with her.
A lot is lost, but I can tell you more
about your family, Ottar, stupid boy!

22.   And Isolf, Asolf, Olmoð's sons, as well,
and Skurhild, Skekkil's only daughter, too,
their names are known as mighty warriors,
and they're your family, Ottar, stupid boy!

23.   Gunnarr the Ridge and Grim, Carver of Ploughs,
        Þorir Iron-Shield and Ulf the Gaper,

24.   Bui, Brami, Barri, Reifnir, too,
        Tind and Tyrfing and the Hadding boys,
        they're all your family, Ottar, stupid boy!

25.   The sons of Arngrim and of Eyfura,
        An and Om, were born in eastern lands.
        The stories of berserkers' vile deeds
        then spread across the land like wildfire,
        and they're your family, Ottar, stupid boy!

26.   I knew both Brodd and Horvi when they were
        a part of Hrolf the Old's great retinue,
        and all the children born to Jormunrekk,
        by marriage he was one of Sigurð's kin,
        the bane of armies, Fafnir's final foe.

27.   That hero bore the blood of Volsung's line,
        as Hrauðung blood flowed through his mother's veins,
        and Eylim was a son of Auðling's clan,
        and they're your family, Ottar, stupid boy!

28.   And Hogni and Gunnar of the Gjukung clan,
        their sister Guðrun, Gjuki's little girl,
        and Guthorm, who was Gjuki's son as well,
        although he did not bear his father's blood,
        they're all your family, Ottar, stupid boy!

29.   And Harald War-Tooth, son of Hrorek, who
        was known to throw his rings, and son of Auð,
        and Auð the Wealthy One was Ivar's girl,
        she married Raðbarð, and gave birth to Randver,
        they all were mortals who were blessed by gods;
        and they're your family, Ottar, stupid boy!

30.   There were a total of eleven gods
        when Baldr sank below the mound of death,
        and Vali swore that he'd avenge this act,
        through Hoð's demise was justice fairly earned,
        and they're your family, Ottar, stupid boy!

31.   Now Baldr's father was the heir of Bur,
        and Frey had married Gerð, who's Gymir's girl,
        of fiendish blood, and born to Aurboð's line,
        and also Þjazi was their relative,
        that shifty devil, who was Skaði's dad.

32.   I've said a lot, and I can tell you more,
        for there is much I know; shall I go on?

33.   Now Haki was the best of Hvæðna's sons,
        and Hvæðna's father's name was Hjorvarð, boy,
        while Heið and Hrossþjolf were Hrimnir's kin.

34.   Now every seer is of Viðolf's blood,
        and every wizard is of Vilmeið's line,
        and wise men too belong to Svarthof's clan,
        and every devil is of Ymir's kin.

35.   I've said a lot, and I can tell you more,
        for there is much I know; shall I go on?

36.   A single man was birthed in ancient times,
        of godly kin, with strength like none have seen.
        Nine women bore this ever-valiant man,
        nine devil-women, at the edge of Earth.

37.   I've said a lot, and I can tell you more,
        for there is much I know; shall I go on?

38.   His mothers' names were Gjalp and Greip and Imð,
        Ulfrun, Eistla, Eyrgjafa as well,
        Atla, Angeyja, and Jarnsaxa.

39.   He got his strength from power of the earth,
        and freezing sea and offered blood of boars.

40.   I've said a lot, and I can tell you more,
        for there is much I know; shall I go on?

41.   With Angrboða Loki birthed a wolf,
        and sired Sleipnir with the seed of Svaðilfari,
        his daughter, though, was seen as worst of all.

42.   A woman burnt her heart on linden wood
and Loki thought he'd found a tasty snack.
He ate the heart, and then it knocked him up,
and from that child every monster came.

43.   The stormy sea will strike against the sky,
and drown the lands, and then the heavens break,
then vicious winds and endless snow will come,
and then, as fate's decreed, the gods will fall.

44.   There was a man, the greatest one of all,
who got his strength from power of the earth.
They called him everywhere the Prosperous Prince,
for he was bound by blood to every throne.

45.   Another man will come, the greatest yet,
although I dare not speak his name aloud![53]
For there are very few who see beyond
the day that Oðin goes to face the wolf."

Freyja said:

46.   "Now give my boar the memory-ale,
so he remembers all he's heard
three days from now, when he competes
in family lore with Angantyr!"

Hyndla said:

47.   "Get out! I'm tired and I want to sleep,
you'll get no further benefit from me!
My dearest friend, you run around in heat
at night like Heiðrun chases billy-goats!

48.   You always run around in horny rage,
there's been a lot of thrusting in your skirt!
My dearest friend, you run around in heat
at night like Heiðrun chases billy-goats!

Freyja said:

49.   "I'll strike you now with devils' flame,
so you don't run away from here!"

---

[53] A likely reference to Jesus.

Hyndla said:

50.   "Your fire burns, the earth is now ablaze,
       I see that most will suffer loss of life!
       I'll bring for Ottar poison mixed with beer,
       and when he drinks it, he will suffer ill!"

Freyja said:

51.   "Your curses can't control a thing,
       I know your threats are empty words!
       He'll only have a helpful drink!
       Great gods, please come to Ottar's aid!"

Rígsþula

Rig's List

Introduction

Rígspula "Rig's List" is found only in the 14th-century *Codex Wormianus* manuscript. The poem is missing its ending, though a rough understanding of it can be guessed from other sources.

What remains of its plot follows the fathering of the three Norse social classes by a god named Rig, and his mentorship of one of his descendants, also named Rig, into a model king. This god is said to be Heimdall by its prose intro, though Rig in the poem has more in common with Oðin; a wandering philanderer associated with runes who patronizes the ruling classes. It is possible the original poet had Oðin in mind, not Heimdall, and that Rig was misidentified by a a later writer, perhaps under influence of *Vøluspá*'s description of humans as "Heimdall's sons".

Rígspula bears all the hallmarks of a praise poem. Its preserved portions begin by justifying the Norse social hierarchy via horrific racist and classist stereotypes, before moving on to glorifying the younger Rig as an ideal king. Its lost ending presumably has Rig found a royal house, whose descendants must be the subjects of the poem's praise. This house is likely the Danish royal family, who are known from other sources to claim descent from a man named Rig. However, the poet himself was likely not of Danish origin, as his work shows some signs of Celtic influence; the name Rig is likely of Irish origin, and his habit of sleeping with his hosts' wives seems to reflect a Celtic tradition in which kings had the right to sleep with their host's wife or daughter. This suggests its poet may have come from the Norse settlements in Ireland or Britain. As these no longer existed after the late 11th century, the poem in likely no younger than that, and may date from as early as the 10th century.

In ancient stories, it was said that a certain god by the name of Heimdall was traveling along the shore, and came to a farmstead, where he introduced himself as Rig. The following poem is based on that story.

1.   In ancient days there walked on verdant roads
a wise and mighty god named Rig.

2.   He wandered far along the middle road
and found a house, its door ajar.
He went inside, and found an open flame,
and seated there, in dated clothes,
an older married couple: Ai and Edda.

3.   Now Rig was wise in matters of the tongue,
and sat between them in the seats
with each of them on either side of him.

4.   Then Edda gifted him a husky loaf,
quite dense and thick, and full of seeds.
A calf was boiled, table set with broth
they had themselves a lovely meal.
Then Rig arose, and felt the need to sleep.

5.   Now Rig was wise in matters of the tongue,
he slept between them in the bed
with each of them on either side of him.

6.   Three days and nights he was a guest of theirs,
then left along the middle road,
and then nine times the lunar cycles passed.

7.   Then Edda bore a son with skin like pitch.
They sprinkled him[54] and named him Slave.

---

[54] Sprinkling babies' heads with water was a genuine pagan practice; based on the context here, perhaps as part of a naming ceremony. The similarity to Christian baptism is probably coincidental.

8.   The boy grew up, became a healthy man
        with wrinkled skin upon his hands,
        with twisted knuckles and a crooked back,
        with fingers thick and gangly heels,
        and with a face as ugly as could be.

9.   And then the man began to test his strength,
        he bound the bast and carried burdens,
        and carried firewood for all his days.

10.   A girl with crooked legs came to his yard,
        her feet were filthy, arms were burnt,
        and nose was bent; she said her name was Maid.

11.   She came inside and sat between the seats,
        beside her sat the family's son.
        They softly spoke, and then they made the bed,
        did Slave and Maid, for all their days.

12.   They settled down, were happy, and had sons,
        Their names were Barn and Bawler-Boy,
        Horsefly, Stinky, Rough, and Concubine,
        and Clumsy, Grizzly, Stump and Fat,
        Hunch-Back, Bow-Leg; and all of them laid fences,
        they kept the pigs and tended goats,
        they dug the turf and lined the fields with shit.

13.   They named their daughters Pudge and Lady-Stump,
        and Thunder-Thigh and Eagle-Nose,
        Handmaid, Screamer, Oaken-Stick,
        Ragged-Dress and Heron-Legs;
        and every slave who's lived has borne their blood.

14.   But Rig continued on the rightward road,
        and found a hall with open doors.
        He went inside, and found an open flame,
        and married people, working hard.

15.   The man was carving wood for weaving-beams,
        His beard was clean, his hair cut short,
        his shirt fit well; a box was on the floor.

16.   The woman sat, and made the distaff spin,
        she stretched her arms, and readied cloth.
        She wore an angled bonnet and a smock,
        a scarf and clasps upon her shoulders.
        They gave their names as Afi and Amma.

17.   Now Rig was wise in matters of the tongue,
        and sat between them in the seats
        with each of them on either side of him.

[It appears a stanza is missing here, based on the pattern of the
other two visits. Presumably Amma gives Rig food of middling
quality.]

18.   Then Rig arose, for he had need to sleep,
        and laid between them in the bed,
        with each of them on either side of him.

19.   Three days and nights he was a guest of theirs,
        then left along the middle road,
        and then nine times the lunar cycles passed.

20.   Then Amma bore a son with ruddy skin.
        They sprinkled him and named him Man,
        his eyes went back and forth as he was swaddled.

21.   The boy grew up, became a healthy man,
        he sculpted homes and crafted barns,
        he tamed the oxen and he readied plows,
        then drove the plows, and made the carts.

22.   And then a bride came home with hanging keys,
        her name was In-Law, dressed in skins,
        she donned the linen veil, and married Man.
        They settled down, exchanged their jewelry,
        they made the bed, began a family.

23.   They settled down, were happy, and had sons
        named Man and Badass, Thane and Smith,
        Landowner, Broad and Farmer, Braided Beard,
        Neighbor, Landsman, Tall-Beard, Soldier.

24.	They named their daughters many things as well:
Slender, Proud and Girl and Bride,
Sparky, Woman, Shy and Vicious, Wife,
and every peasant family's borne their blood.

25.	But Rig continued on the rightward road,
and found a manor, facing south,
the door was cracked, a ring hung from the post.

26.	He entered, saw the floor was lined with straw,
saw staring in each other's eyes
and fiddling with their fingers were Faðir and Moðir.

27.	The man was seated, tying strings to bows,
he bent the elm, and arrows fletched.
The woman fretted much about her arms,
she stroked her robe and fluffed the sleeves.

28.	She wore a headdress and an azure shirt,
a necklace and a flowing dress.
Her brows were shining, and her chest as well,
her neck was white as fallen snow.

29.	Now Rig was wise in matters of the tongue,
and sat between them in the seats
with each of them on either side of him.

30.	Then Moðir took a fancy linen cloth
and put it on the tabletop.
The loaves she served were thin and shining white,
for they were made of perfect wheat.
She set the silverware and dishes full
of boiled pork and roasted birds.
She filled the cups, they had a lot of wine,
and all day long they drank and talked.

31.	Now Rig was wise in matters of the tongue,
he rose, and then he made the bed,
three days and nights he was a guest of theirs,
then left along the middle road,
and then nine times the lunar cycles passed.

32.   Then Móðir bore a son, she swaddled him
and sprinkled him, and named him Jarl.
His hair was blond, his cheeks were bright,
his eyes were evil like a snake's.

33.   And Jarl grew up, became a healthy man.
He shattered shields and strung his bows,
he bent the elm, and fletched his arrows too.
He wielded spears, and let them fly,
he learned to ride a horse, unleash his hounds,
to use a sword, to swim the fjords.

34.   Then Rig arrived from deep within the woods,
he met with Jarl and taught him runes.
He said, "I see you are a worthy son,
so you may share the name of Rig!
Go build a kingdom from the ancient fields!"

35.   And so he rode across the frosty peaks
and murky woods, until he reached a hall.
He wielded spears, and shook his shield,
he struck his horse and drew his sword.
He started wars and watered fields with blood,
by slaying men he won his lands.

36.   In total he ruled over eighteen lands
and shared his wealth with everyone.
His precious treasures, and his slender steeds,
his rings and bracelets too were shared.

37.   He sent his runners over soggy roads
to reach the hall where Hersir lived.
They met a lovely girl with slender fingers
and wisdom wide; her name was Erna.

38.   They got her hand, and brought her back to Jarl,
she donned the veil and married him.
They settled down, began a family,
and lived content and happy lives.

39. [55] Their elder sons were Burr and Barn and Joð,
       Aðal, Arfi, Mog as well,
       the next were Nið and Niðjung, they could play,
       then Son and Svein, who swam and gamed,
       then Kund came next, and Kon, the youngest one.

40.   The sons of Jarl grew up as healthy men,
       they tended horses, bound their shields,
       they crafted arrows, and they shook their spears.

41.   But Kon, the youngest, had a gift for runes,
       eternal runes and runes of life,
       The runes for saving men, and blunting blades,
       and runes to calm a stormy sea.

42.   He understood the birds, could calm a flame,
       could still the sea, relieve depression,
       he matched eight men in strength and energy.

43.   He dueled with Rig-Jarl over all the runes
       and showed his mastery of tricks.
       He won the victory, the name of Rig,
       and all the secrets of the runes.

44.   One morning Kon was riding through the woods,
       his arrows silencing the birds,
       when from a branch a crow called out to him,

45.   "Why do you waste your life by shooting birds?
       You should be riding off to war,
       destroying armies, mounted on your horse!

46.   I know that Dan and Danp have grand estates,
       more so than anything you have.
       They're master sailors, mighty swordsmen, too,
       they injure men like no one else!"

[55] Most of these names mean *son, boy, kinsman,* or something along those lines.

The manuscript cuts off abruptly at this point, and so the poem is incomplete. According to the *Skjoldunga Saga*, Rig goes on to marry Danp's daughter and found the royal line of Denmark, so presumably the rest of the poem described these events.

Gróttasøngr

The Song of Grotti

Introduction

Gróttasøngr "Grotti's Song" is preserved in several manuscripts of the *Prose Edda*, along with a lengthy prose text providing background for its events. The prose introduction in this book is edited based on this description. The basic story also survived in Scandinavian folklore through the 19th century.

It purports to be a working song sung by a pair of fiends enslaved by the Danish king Fróði as they grind a magical millstone for him.

Some manuscripts of the *Prose Edda* state that the whirlpool formed by Grotti in the ending is the Swelkie whirlpool in Orkney, which may suggest that the poem was composed there, as a legend about the Swelkie's origin would have been very prominent for its people. Some of the poem's vocabulary is otherwise found only in Christian texts, suggesting a post-conversion date in the late 11th or 12th centuries.

Froði, son of Friðleif, was king of the lands now called Denmark, but which once were called Gotland. He inherited the kingdom at the same time Augustus ruled Rome, and when Christ was born. Because Froði was the strongest king in the North at the time, the great peace was attributed to him, and called Froði's Peace by the people of the northern lands. No one hurt another, even if he happened to meet a man who killed his kin. There were no thieves or robbers, and a gold ring could sit out in the open a long time without being taken.

Froði once went to a festival hosted by Fjolnir, who was king of Sweden at the time. While there, he bought two slave-girls named Fenja and Menja, who were big and strong.

Around this time two great millstones were found in Denmark, so large that no one could move them. These stones had the ability to grind out whatever the grinder wished for. This mill was named Grotti. Froði ordered his new slaves to work the mill and to grind out gold, peace, and happiness for him. As they ground, it's said they sang this song, which is now called the *Song of Grotti*:

1. Fenja and Menja, far of sight,
    had come to Froði's house.
    The son of Friðleif held them fast
    as captives in his home.

2. He led them to the flour-mill
    and ordered it be turned.
    He swore they'd get no rest or sleep
    before he heard their song.

3. They sang a song unceasingly,
    their voices never stilled.
    "Please let us set the mill aside
    and give the stone a break!"
    But Froði ordered once again
    that they must never stop.

4.   They kept on singing as they ground
and turned the twisting stone.
Though Froði's other workers slept,
their grinding never ceased.
Then Menja spoke as flour came
at last from Grotti's stones.

5.   "Let's grind for Froði wealth and bliss
upon the joyous mill!
He'll sit on gold and sleep on down
and wake a happy man!

6.   May no one harm his fellow man
with words or biting blades,
not even if his brother's killer
is bound in front of him!"

7.   But Froði only said to them,
"You'll rest as long as cuckoos sing
or noise departs my mouth."

8.   "It seems that Froði's not so wise
when he selects his slaves!
He picked us for our looks and strength,
but did not ask our kin.

9.   For strong were Hrungnir and his dad,
and Þjazi stronger still.
Our brothers' names are Ið and Aurn,
for we are mountain-fiends.

10.   And Grotti would have never come
from out of Griafjall,
nor would a devil grind a mill
if we knew not of it.

11.   Nine years we lived beneath the earth,
and always played together.
We moved the mountain-throne away
along with other deeds.

12.   We brought the stone to fiendish lands,
it caused the earth to shake.
We flung the mighty stone so far
that humans found it first.

13.   And since we were in Sweden then,
we both went off to war!
We baited bears and shattered shields,
and fought an armored force.

14.   We helped one prince destroy another,
and Guthorm got our aid.
There was no peace or merriment
until Knui fell.

15.   We lived as soldiers quite a while,
and heroes we were called.
Our spears drew blood from grievous wounds,
our swords were painted red.

16.   Now we have come to Froði's house
as slaves, with no respect!
Our feet are swallowed by the mud,
our heads are freezing cold.
Yet we must always turn the stone,
for Froði's house is cruel.

17.   My hands must rest, the stone must stop,
for I have ground enough!"
"We cannot stop our grinding now,"
said Fenja to her mate,
"Till Froði feels we've ground enough,
our hands must never rest.

18.   For hands must handle hardy spears
and stain them red with blood!
The king must soon wake up to hear
our songs and ancient tales.

19.   A fire's burning in the east,
for war is now awake!
An army comes to burn the hall
in front of Froði's eyes.

20.   He will not hold the Danish throne,
nor rings, nor holy stones!
Now grind with all your might, my girl,
for gore won't slow us down.

21.   My father's daughter ground with force
when she foresaw much death.
The iron rods came off the mill,
but we have more to grind!"

22.   The son of Yrsa, Halfdan's kin,
will slaughter Froði soon.
He'll be her brother and her son,[56]
so let us grind some more!

23.   The girls then ground with all their might,
their fiendish rage immense,
the timbers cracked, the stand was dropped,
the heavy stone was split.

24.   "We've milled for Froði long enough,
and now it's time to stop!
Enough of life we've wasted here
but now we girls are free!"

They ground a hostile army for Froði, and that night the pirate Mysing killed Froði and sacked his capital, and thus ended Froði's peace. Among Mysing's booty were Grotti, Fenja, and Menja, and he ordered them to grind salt. They did this a while before the ship sank. Then a great whirlpool formed in the sea where the water met the center of the millstone, and that's why the sea is salty.

---

[56] This refers to the legendary king Hrolf Kraki, who is both Yrsa's son and brother as she inadvertently married her father.

Vǫlundarkviða

Wayland's Wrath

Introduction

Vǫlundarkviða "Wayland's Poem" is preserved in full in the *Codex Regius,* and the beginning of its prose intro is also found in AM 748 I 4to. The poem tells a Norse variant of a common Germanic legend of Wayland the Smith, which is also found in the Norse *Þiðreks Saga,* a translation of German heroic traditions, and alluded to in various Old English poems and artworks. *Vǫlundarkviða* is the only poetic version of this story to survive.

Though details vary, the basic story of all of these is of a talented smith who is hobbled and kidnapped by a greedy king, and who then takes bloody revenge ad escapes.

Vǫlundarkviða is likely an older poem; its many indications of Old English influence suggest an origin in the Danelaw, the Norse-colonized area of eastern England. This settlement began in the mid-9th century and had largely stopped by the end of the 10th, suggesting that the poem was composed in this time frame.

There was a king in Sweden named Niðuð. He had two sons and a daughter, whose name was Boðvild.

There were also three brothers, the sons of a Sami king. The eldest was Slagfið, the second Egil, and the youngest was Wayland. They went to Ulfdalir and built a house near the lake of Ulfsjar. One morning they saw three valkyries sitting by the shore, spinning linen, their swan-cloaks beside them. Two of them were Svanhvit and Alvit, daughters of Hloðver, while the third was Olrun, daughter of Kjar of Valland.

They took the girls home, and each married one; Slagfið married Svanhvit, Egil married Olrun, and Wayland married Alvit. They lived together seven years, and then the girls flew off, looking for battle, and never returned. Slagfið and Egil left in search of their wives, but Wayland stayed behind.

As everyone knows from the old stories, Wayland was the most skilled man in all the lands. Niðuð once kidnapped him, as is told here.

1. Three ladies flew across the murky woods,
   for that was where they'd find their fate.
   They found a resting place beside the sea,
   and started weaving linen threads.

2. Then one of them, the loveliest of all,
   wrapped Egil in her shining arms.
   The second, Svanhvit, bore the wings of swans.
   The third, their sister, also wound
   her arms 'round Wayland's pearly neck.

3. They lived together seven happy years,
   but on the eighth they yearned for war,
   and on the ninth desire parted them,
   they flew across the murky woods,
   for that was where they felt they'd find their fate.

4. And when the men returned from hunting game
   they found their halls, but no one home.
   Then in and out and all around they looked,
   and east went Egil, after Olrun,
   and south went Slagfið, hot on Svanhvit's trail.

5. But Wayland stayed behind in Ulfdalir,
  encircled shining gems with gold.
  He fashioned gorgeous rings in serpents' shape
  and waited long to see the day
  the girl he loved would come back home to him.

6. But soon the news reached Niðuð, Njara's king,
  that Wayland now was on his own.
  By night his army reached the hall,
  their shields all shimmered in the waning moon.

7. The king dismounted at the gable-doors
  and wandered all across the hall.
  Upon a rope of bast he saw the rings,
  eight hundred forty, Wayland made.

8. He took them off the rope, admired them,
  then put them back, except for one.
  Then Wayland came back home from hunting game,
  he'd traveled far, and sought to rest.

9. And so he sat to cook a bear he'd killed,
  the arid wood cast crimson through the hall
  in front of Wayland's weary eyes.

10. The elvish prince sat down to count his rings,
  and found that one had disappeared.
  He hoped his wife had come and taken one,
  and that at last his heart could heal.

11. He waited for her till he fell asleep,
  and then awoke without his will!
  His hands were weighted down with massive chains,
  his feet were fastened to the floor.

12. He said, "What sort of men are you, who've bound
  me in my home with ropes of bast?"

13. Then Niðuð, Njara's king, called out to him,
  "Now tell us, wisest of the elves,
  how did you gather all this wealth for us?"

14. "There surely was no gold on Grani's path,
     the Rhine is far away from here.[57]
     These treasures don't compare to those I had
     when I still had a family here."

15. Then Niðuð's wife came pacing through the hall,
     then told her man, in whispered voice:
     "That forest-man seems so uncivilized!"

King Niðuð gave Boðvild, his daughter, the gold ring he had stolen from
Wayland's bast-rope. Niðuð himself took Wayland's sword. Then the
queen said:

16. "You see, he snarls when he sees the sword
     or when we show him Boðvild's ring!
     His eyes are cold and empty like a snake's,
     I say we cut his hamstrings out
     and leave him hobbled by the shore!"

And so it was done. Wayland's hamstrings were cut, and he was exiled to
a coastal island called Saevarstað. There he made treasures of all sorts for
the king. No one except Niðuð would dare go anywhere near him.

17. He said, "My sword is shining on his belt,
     it was the sharpest one I made!
     That blade was tempered with my finest arts,
     but Niðuð bears it far away.
     I'll never mend that shining blade again!

18. And Boðvild has the scarlet ring I made
     my wife; I swear I'll have revenge!"

19. He lit the forge and hammered, never slept,
     and fashioned Niðuð wondrous things.
     And then, one day, the king brought family,
     his sons were hyped to see the forge.

---

[57] Niðuð implicitly accuses Wayland of stealing gold from him, and Wayland counters by
calling the king's wealth unimpressive. Grani is the horse of the hero Sigurð, whose
famous hoard features prominently later in this book.

20.   They went to Wayland's chest, and got the key,
and marveled at the things he'd made.
They did not know they'd opened ill intent
when Niðuð's sons looked in the chest.

21.   He said, "Come back tomorrow, boys!
I'll show you everything I've got!
Come by yourselves, and speak a word to none,
not man or maid, you're coming here!"

22.   They got up early, and were in a rush
to see the rest of Wayland's works,
they went back to the chest, and got the key,
but all they found was Wayland's wrath.

23.   A single stroke removed the children's heads!
He hid their legs beneath his forge,
he gave the bowls that laid beneath their hair
to Niðuð, with a silver skin.

24.   He hardened diamonds from their shining eyes
and gifted them to Niðuð's wife,
he lastly crafted pendants from their teeth
which went 'round Boðvild's pearly neck.

25.   Then Boðvild came to him about the ring,
she broke it, but she sang its praise,
she said, "I badly need this ring repaired,
there's none I trust with it but you!"

26.   Then Wayland said "I'll fix it easily,
you'll never know the crack was there!
Your dad will say it's better than before,
your mom will say it's prettier."

27.   He gave her beer until she fell asleep,
his wit was greater than a girl's.
"At last, my wrongs have been avenged," he said,
"except for one, which calls for worse!

28.   I would be well if I could use my fins
        which Niðuð stole away from me!"
        Then, laughing, Wayland rose into the air[58]
        while Boðvild left in tears; her love was gone,
        and now she feared her father's wrath.

29.   The cunning wife of Niðuð stood outside,
        she'd paced across the hall's expanse,
        she found him slumped against the wall, and asked,
        "Are you awake, Niðuð, my love?"

30.   He said, "I'm always up, I've lost my will,
        without my sons, I cannot sleep.
        My head is cold, and so are all your words,
        I'll hear what Wayland has to say."

31.   "Now tell me, Wayland, wisest of the elves,
        What happened to my little cubs?"

32.   "First, I ask you swear an oath to me
        by hull of ship and rim of shield,
        by haunch of horse and edge of blade,
        That you won't harm the mother of my son,
        or be the cause of her demise,
        whether or not she's someone that you know
        or if he's born within your hall!

33.   You'll find them at the forge you made for me,
        you'll find the bags are stained with blood!
        I slaughtered them, they're shorter by a head,
        and buried them beneath the flame!

34.   Their skulls produced those lovely silver bowls
        I sent your Highness just today!
        The diamonds too, the ones I sent your wife,
        your sons once used them all to see!

---

[58] In other versions of this story, Wayland is able to fly using artifical wings he built during his enslavement. Here, his flight may be magical, owing to his elven nature.

168

35.   Those pendants, too, the ones that Boðvild got,
        I fashioned them from all their teeth!
        I gave her something else as well;
        your only daughter's swollen with my son!"

36.   "There's nothing you can say to hurt me more,
        and if you could, I could not stop you!
        There's none so tall to knock you off a horse
        and none whose shots could shoot you down
        from where you're hiding, high within the clouds!"

37.   The smith flew off, his laugh like thunder's boom,
        but Niðuð, bitter, stayed behind.

38.   "Get up now, Þakkrað, finest of my slaves,
        go get my daughter, get her dressed
        in all her finest clothes to meet her dad!"

39.   "Were Wayland's words the truth, my girl?
        Did you submit to him?"

40.   "His words were true, my lord,
        he forced me in his forge
        an agonizing hour!
        It never should have been,
        I could not fight him off,
        he was too strong for me!"

Heroic Poems
Tales of Adventure, Valor, and Tragedy

Hervararkviða

Angantyr's Awakening

Introduction

The next two poems in this book are a unique case among the poems of the Edda; they are not preserved independently in any manuscript, but are instead excerpts from an Icelandic saga, *Hervarar Saga ok Heiðreks*. This saga, like most, is written mainly in prose, with some dialogue in verse. However, these sections are noteworthy for having extensive sections in verse, which has led to some speculation that they may have once been separate poems, roughly integrated into the saga.

The first of these poems follows Hervor, one of the saga's protagonists, visiting her father's grave to retrieve the cursed sword Tyrfing from his corpse. This segment received attention from scholars very early in the history of the study of Norse literature, and was in fact the first Eddic poem to be translated into English. It was noticed that this section works quite well as an independent story from the saga, and combined with its minimal prose and extended verse dialogue has caused many to suspect that it may have once existed as a separate poem, which modern editors have titled *Hervararkviða* "Hervor's Poem".

Hervarar Saga was likely compiled in the 12th or 13th century, so the poem is surely older than that. It has no especially early features to it, either, so it may date from the 10th or 11th century.

1.   At dusk a girl arrived in Munarvag
and there she found a shepherd tending sheep.

He said:

2.   "What sort of fool would travel here alone?
You'd best depart, and find a place to stay!"

She said:

3.   "I won't depart, or find a place to stay,
for I don't know the island's wild men.
I need to know, before I take my leave:
Where are the barrows bearing Hjorvarð's name?"

He said:

4.   "No man who's wise would ask me such a thing,
my Viking friend, I think you've gone astray!
We need to leave, as fast as we can go,
for evil beings dwell outside at night.

5.   You are a fool if you would travel there
alone, through murky darkness and the barrow flames!
The tombs are open, raging fires burn
the fields and fens; I'm telling you, depart!"

She said:

6.   "I'll pay you with a golden amulet,
but know your words will never hold me back.
There are no gleaming rings or shining gems
that will delay my journey to the graves.

7.   I do not fear the roaring flames of death
not even if they eat the island whole!
I will not flee for fear of spirits' wrath,
so, coward, tell me what I want to know!"

8.   And then the shepherd ran into the woods,
the woman's words he had to flee in haste.
The sturdy heart inside the woman's chest
was swollen greatly at the fool's escape.

Then she saw that out on the island the flames of the dead were burning, and she went to them without fear, even though all the grave-mounds were around her. She went through the fire as if it were nothing at all, until she reached the berserkers' barrow.

Then she shouted:

9. "Awaken, Angantyr! For Hervor calls,
the only daughter Svava had with you!
I've come to claim the brutal blade you bore,
the dwarven-smelted sword of Sigrlami.

10. Hervarð, Hjorvarð, Hrani, Angantyr!
Wake up and rise from underneath the roots,
with helmets, armor, and your keenest blades,
with harnesses and shields, and sharpened spears.

11. The sons of Arngrim now are much reduced,
and I will know they've now increased the earth,
if silence is the hospitality
I get from all the sons of Eyfura.[59]

12. Hervarð, Hjorvarð, Hrani, Angantyr!
May all of you feel nothing in your ribs
but vile rot as maggots eat your flesh
if I can't have the sword that Dvalin smithed,
a sword like that's too good for ghosts to bear."

Then Angantyr said:

13. "My daughter, Hervor, why awaken me?
That blade will lead you to an evil doom!
You've lost your mind, your wisdom's clearly gone
if you, with wicked thoughts, would rouse the dead.

14. I was not buried by my family.
Two warriors stole Tyrfing off my corpse
and only one still lives to wield it now."

---

[59] This line suggests that ghosts were believed to cease to exist when the body had fully decomposed.

Hervor said:

15.   "You lie! May you be cursed by all the gods
to never rot, if you don't have the blade!
I think you fear to give your only heir
the patrimony that she's rightly earned."

Then the barrow opened, and fire erupted out of it, and engulfed the land around the grave. Then Angantyr said:

16.   "The gate of hell is lifted, mounds are open,
and flames are swallowing the island whole!
Around my grave right now are evil sights,
go to your ship, as fast as you can run!"

Hervor said:

17.   "You cannot pierce the night with flame so bright
that it will scare me, or will make me flee!
My heart will never waver, even if
I see a spirit standing in the door!

18.   Again, I curse you, corpses of my kin,
to be intact forever in your graves
among the ghosts, half-rotten, evermore,
unless I get from Angantyr the blade
that shatters shields, that's known as Hjalmar's bane."

Angantyr said:

19.   "You are inhuman, daughter of my flesh,
you skulk near barrows under veil of night
with bloodied spears and mail of Gothic make
and fully armored near the doors of death."

Hervor said:

20.   "Indeed, a human I was thought to be
till here I traveled, looking for your hall.
Now give to me the armor-hating blade
that shatters shields, that's known as Hjalmar's bane."

Angantyr said:

21. "The bane of Hjalmar lies beneath my back,
and all around it's wrapped with dancing flame.
I've never known a girl in all the world
who's brave enough to hold this evil blade."

Hervor said:

22. "I swear, I'll keep the cursed sword in hand,
if I can get it, I will keep it close.
I do not fear the flame that veils the blade,
in fact, it dims the more it meets my gaze."

Angantyr said:

23. "For all your courage, daughter, you're a fool
to walk into the flame with open eyes!
I'll fetch the sword myself, and hand it over,
I see you are too stubborn to refuse."

Hervor said:

24. "You've done the noble thing, my Viking kin,
to place your sword into my custody.
I'd rather have this precious blade in hand
than all of Norway under my command."

Angantyr said:

25. "You do not understand your evil words,
you stupid girl, you should not celebrate!
For Tyrfing, daughter, hear what I must say,
will be the ruin of your family.

26. I've seen the threads of fate, and I can tell
of what the future holds for you, my girl.
For Tyrfing, daughter, hear what I must say,
will be the ruin of your family.

27. You'll bear a son, who'll wield it after you,
he'll brandish Tyrfing and will trust his strength.
You'll call him Heiðrek, he'll be widely famed
beneath the sun, the greatest of mankind."

Hervor said:

28.   "And now I'll take my leave, my ship awaits,
but know you've made your daughter very glad.
And father, know I do not give a damn
about the future that awaits my sons."

Angantyr said:

29.   "I know you'll keep the blade for many years,
and keep it safe within a hidden place.
Don't touch the blade, its edge is poison-laced,
the death it brings is worse than words can say.

30.   Farewell, my daughter, know I'd sooner give
to you the health and strength of twelve berserkers
and all the wealth that Arngrim's sons have left
than see you leave with that accursed blade."

Hervor said:

31.   "May you and all your brothers rest in peace
beneath the earth, but now I must depart.
I've stood between the lands of life and death
too long, with fire on my every side."

Hløðskviða

The Battle of the Goths and Huns

Introduction

The second poem to be derived from *Hervarar Saga*'s verse sections, *Hløðskviða* "Hloð's Poem" has been preserved in much worse shape than its predecessor. The remaining verses are interspersed with lengthy segments of prose, and many words are difficult to interpret and may be corrupt.

The poem takes place well after the events of *Hervararkviða*, and details the struggle of Hervor's grandsons, Hloð and Angantyr, over the inheritance of their father, Heiðrek, Hervor's son. These events are also alluded to in the Old English poem *Widsiþ*, which gives names very similar to those of this poem's characters (compare Old English *Heaðoric*, *Incgenþeow*, and *Hliþ* with Old Norse *Heiðrek*, *Angantýr*, and *Hløðr*).

Hløðskviða likely contains the oldest verses in this book. It seems to be based on oral recollections of the wars between the Goths and Huns in the 4th and 5th centuries, and it preserves many names of both places and tribes that appear to be of genuine Eastern European origin, and which would have been foreign to even the oldest Norseman. Its verse is also much looser than that of later poems, allowing much more variation in both the number and patterning of syllables per line than later poetry, where the syllabic restrictions are much tighter. This suggests the surviving verses may be from as early as the 6th century, though the 7th or 8th are perhaps more likely.

1.   In early days, when Humli ruled the Huns,
        and Gizur Gauts, and Angantyr the Goths,
        and Valdar Danes, and Kjar[60] in Rome
        and Alrek ruled the valiant English men,

2.   in Hunnish lands did Hloð depart the womb
        with dagger, blade, and fully clad in mail,
        with savage sword and helm adorned with rings,
        and horses tamed within the holy woods.

Now Hloð had learned of Heiðrek's death, and that his brother Angantyr had become king of all their father's lands. He and Humli decided that he should go and demand his share of the inheritance from Angantyr with kind words.

3.   Then Hloð, the son of Heiðrek, traveled west
        to Arheim, where the Goths had made their home,
        to claim the lands his blood had given hm
        where Angantyr was toasting Heiðrek's name.

4.   He found a soldier standing by the door,
        he hailed the man, and made demands of him:
        "Go in, my friend, and greet king Angantyr,
        and make my brother come and speak with me!"

The man went to the king's table, greeted him warmly, and said:

5.   "The Hunnish son of Heiðrek has arrived,
        your bastard brother, fully geared for war.
        He's fierce and proud upon his mighty horse
        and says, my lord, he's come to speak with you."

When the king heard, he slammed his knife into the table, then put on his mail-coat and took his gleaming shield in one hand and Tyrfing in the other.

6.   The hall erupted when the prince arose,
        for all were keen to hear the words of Hloð
        and then what answer Angantyr would give.

---

[60] Probably a Norse adaptation of *Caesar*.

Angantyr said:

7. "You're welcome here, my brother, Heiðrek's son,
 come sit beside me on the royal bench!
 Let's drown our grief in Heiðrek's finest drinks
 and toast our father, first among mankind,
 have wine or mead, whichever you prefer."

Hloð said:

8. "I did not travel here to sip your beer,
 I'll take no cup from you, unless I get
 an equal share of all that Heiðrek owned:
 His tools and weapons, treasures like none else,
 his cows and calves, his many roaring mills,
 his slaves and servants, and their many kin,

9. the famous forest, Murkwood it is called,
 the holy grave that stands in Gothic lands,
 the lovely stone upon the Dneiper's bank,
 and half the armor Heiðrek used to own,
 his lands and soldiers and his precious rings."

Angantyr said:

10. "I'll see your shining shield in pieces, boy,
 and frigid spears stained red with scarlet blood
 and many soldiers sink into the grass
 before I halve my wealth with Humli's boy
 or, of my will, see Tyrfing split in two!

11. But shining spears I'll gladly give to you,
 and wealth and cows, if that will keep you calm.
 You'll get twelve hundred slaves from me,
 you'll get twelve hundred steeds from me,
 you'll get twelve hundred servants bearing shields.

12. I'll share my wealth with every man of yours,
 they'll never have a better thing than these!
 I'll give a lovely girl to each of them,
 and each of them will wear a golden chain.

13.   I'll shower you with silver where you sit,
        and when you leave, I'll stuff your steeds with gold,
        and all around you, rings will freely roll,
        I'll let you rule a third of Gothic land."

Gizur, king of the Grytings[61] and Heiðrek's foster father, was also in attendance, despite his great age. He felt that Angantyr had offered his brother too much, and he declared:

14.   "That is the best a son of slaves could have,
        the greatest gain a bastard boy can get!
        Your sat your butt upon a barrow's crest
        while princes split the prizes that they'd earned."

Hloð was enraged at being spoken to in this way, and left immediately, returning to Hunland, to the court of Humli, his mother's father, and told him that his brother had refused to divide their inheritance equally. Humli asked what had happened, and was furious to hear that his grandson had been called a bastard and a slave's son. He said:

15.   "Let's feast and celebrate till winter's end,
        let's plan our war and sip the finest drinks.
        Let's teach the Huns to bear the tools of war
        and boldly use them on the battlefield.

16.   For you, I'll raise an army vast and strong,
        and bravely they will slaughter in your name.
        With boys of twelve and foals of barely two
        will Hunland rise to shield her prince's name."

That whole winter Hloð and Humli were quiet, but when spring came, they mustered a vast army, so huge that all of Hunland was deprived of fighting-age men. When this army had gathered, they marched through Murkwood, the forest which split the Goth and Hun lands. On the other side, they found vast, flat plains, flush with prosperous farms. On the plain was a castle ruled by Hervor, Hloð and Angantyr's sister, and Ormar, her foster father. They had a strong garrison there, ready to ward off any Hunnish attacks.

---

[61] Probably a very archaic name for the Ostrogoths, preserved in Latin sources as *Greutungi*.

186

One morning, as the sun was rising, Hervor went on watch and saw a huge
dust cloud that blocked out the sun. Then she saw a gleam inside the dust,
as if a mountain of gold had appeared on the horizon. She looked closer
and saw that it was no gold, but shields and gilded helmets and mail-coats
gleaming in the lingering sunbeams, and she knew it was a massive
Hunnish army. She called for her trumpeter, and told him to blow his horn
to rally her troops, but told Ormar to ride out and meet the Huns at the
castle's south gate, and challenge them there. Ormar said:

> 17.   "I'll surely ride, with sturdy shield in hand,
>   to war and glory for the Gothic land!"

Then Ormar rode out and called to the Huns, telling them to ride to the
castle's southern gate, and wait there for the Gothic force to meet them in
battle.

Hervor and her army rode out and met the Huns, and a great battle was
fought there. But the Huns' greater numbers won them the day, and they
slaughtered the bulk of Hervor's force. Eventually, Hervor herself fell, and
then her army became terrified and fled. Ormar rode away, day and night,
as hard as he could, to deliver the news to Angantyr in Arheim, while the
Huns were ravaging and burning the countryside. When he arrived before
Angantyr, he said:

> 18.   "I've traveled north to share this news with you:
>   The trees of Murkwood are engulfed in flame,
>   and Gothland's plains are soaked with heroes' blood.

> 19.   I witnessed Hervor, Heiðrek's little girl,
>   your only sister, sink into the grass.
>   The Hunnish spearmen charged and cut her down
>   and thousands more were slaughtered by her side.

> 20.   She was much happier to fight than flirt
>   or sit, a wedded bride, upon a bench."

When he heard this, Angantyr pursed his lips and sat silently, looking over
the few men who remained in his court. After a long while, he said:

> 21.   "A mighty army came to drink my mead,
>   but now that battle's come, their number's shrunk!

22.   I see no savior sitting in my court,
no man to beg for aid or buy with rings,
no man to ride with sturdy shield in hand
to greet the Huns, and challenge them to war."

Then old Gizur said:
23.   "I'll ask for no reward from you,
no clinking coin or single piece of gold.
But I will ride, with sturdy shield in hand,
and cordially invite the Huns to war."

Then Gizur got his best armor and weapons, and mounted his horse as if he were young again. He said:

24.   "Where should I lead the Huns to face our force?"

Angantyr said:
25.   "We'll face them on the mighty Danube's banks
on ashen peaks where Goths have always fought,
where all our fathers earned their famous names,
where glory came from many victories."

Then Gizur rode off until he found the vast Hunnish army. He rode up within earshot of them, then shouted loudly:

26.   "Your legion quakes, your leaders all are doomed,
our banners rise, and Oðin's wrath is roused!

27.   You'll find us on the mighty Danube's banks
we'll battle you beneath the ashen peaks.
May all your dead[62] be seen in every land,
may Oðin guide my spear to those he'll get!"

28.   When Hloð heard Gizur's words, he said:
"Now someone seize the Grytings' chieftain, fast,
he's come from Arheim, fights for Angantyr!"

Humli said:
29.   "We must not harm a man who rides alone."

---

[62] The manuscript has *hái*, which means "dog shark", and is likely a scribal error. The translation of this line is thus partial guesswork.

188

Then Gizur called:

30.   "We do not fear you, or your bows of horn!"

Then Gizur struck his horse and rode back to Angantyr's camp, and greeted him with kind words. Angantyr asked Gizur how big of an army the Huns had mustered. Gizur told him:

31.   "They've six battalions mustered over there,
                there are five companies in each of them,
                each company has thirteen hundred men,
                each hundred truly is four hundred men."

Angantyr, now knowing the size of the enemy force, sent out messengers to every land, asking anyone who could fight to come aid him. Then he marched to the Danube with his army, and found a Hunnish force twice the size of his.

The next day the battle began, and lasted all day, and the next eight days, and more men fell there than could be counted. But each day and night more men arrived to fight for Angantyr, and so the overall size of his army did not change over the battle.

Each day the fighting grew fiercer and more bitter, for the Huns knew that they would be slaughtered to a man if they were defeated, while the Goths were fighting for their freedom, and so they urged each other to keep fighting.

Finally, on the ninth day, the Hunnish lines began to waver, and Angantyr stepped out in front of the Gothic lines, with his bright shield and the famed sword Tyrfing, and led the Goths on the final charge. At this the Hunnish lines broke completely, and the Goths butchered all of them, including Hloð and Humli. They killed so many Huns that the Danube was choked by their corpses, and the valleys around it were stuffed full to bursting with dead men and horses.

Angantyr searched among the dead until he found the corpse of his brother Hloð. He said:

32.   "I offered you a hoard uncountable
                of gold and cows, to bring you endless joy.
                No war would gain you more than I would give
                in land or wealth; it's only laid you low.

33.   The worst of men am I; I've slain my kin!
        A fate most cruel the Norns have carved for us!"

Helgakviða Hjørvarðssonar

The Tale of Helgi, son of Hjorvarð

Introduction

Helgakviða Hjǫrvarðssonar "The Poem of Helgi, son of Hjorvarð" is found in the *Codex Regius,* where it occurs between the two poems of Helgi Hundingsbane. For simplicity's sake, I have moved it before the two Hundingsbane poems.

All three Helgi poems follow essentially the same story, of a mortal hero named Helgi who falls for a valkyrie, kills a powerful king whose name begins with H, and then dies at the hands of that king's avenging family. It seems likely that both this Helgi and Helgi Hundingsbane were once the same character, with the stories diverging as they spread through Scandinavia.

The poem is structured akin to an Icelandic saga, with most of the dialogue in verse while the narration is all in prose, likely suggesting a late date. However, *Hjǫrvarðssonar* seems to also include older material then the Hundingsbane poems; notably, its hero is not of the Volsung clan, but rather an Ylfing. Combined with the lack of any equivalent to Helgi in the German version of the Volsung tales, it seems likely that Helgi was originally from a different family and only later incorporated into the Volsung legend. Thus, while the poem as it exists now is probably late, its verses may be much older, fragments of older poems crudely glued together with prose segments. Based on what is known of the Hundingsbane poems, these verses likely date from the 9th or 10th centuries.

There once was a king named Hjorvarð. He had three wives: one was named Alfhild, and their son was named Heðin. The second was Saerið, and their son was named Humlung. The third was Sinrjoð, and their son was named Hymling.

King Hjorvarð swore that his fourth wife would be the most beautiful woman in the world. He learned of a king named Svafnir, whose daughter, Sigrlin, was the most beautiful of all. He sent Atli, the son of his jarl Iðmund, to ask for Sigrlin's hand for him. He spent a full winter with Svafnir.

Svafnir had an earl named Franmar, who was Sigrlin's foster father. He had a daughter named Alof. He would not consent to Sigrlin's marriage, and so Atli went home.

On his way home, Atli was resting in a grove. A bird was sitting in the branches above him, and it had heard Svafnir's men call Hjorvarð's wives the most beautiful women in the world. The bird began to sing, and Atli listened to its words.

The bird said:

1.   "Have you seen Svafnir's daughter, Sigrlin,
the finest sight in all the lovely world?
And yet the men beneath the tree believe
the wives of Hjorvarð are the finest sights!"

Atli said:

2.   "Wise bird, will you speak more of this
to Atli, Iðmund's son?"

The bird said:

3.   "I will, if you will sacrifice to me
and I may have my pick of Hjorvarð's wealth!"

Atli said:

4.   "Do not choose Hjorvarð or his sons,
and not his lovely wives.
Let us negotiate a deal,
for that's the way of friends!"

The bird said:

5.   "I ask for temples, and a holy shrine,
I ask for Hjorvarð's cows with golden horns,
if Sigrlin will sleep in Hjorvarð's arms
and of her own volition goes with him."

This was before Atli had traveled. When he returned and the king asked him how things went, he said:

6.   "We suffered hardship, and we failed.
Our horses tired in the peaks,
and then we had to wade the Saemorn.
Yet still we were denied
the lovely girl you sought."

The king ordered a second delegation sent, and he led it himself. When they came over the mountains, they saw Swabia ablaze and filled with horse-smoke. They rode down and camped by the river. Atli went scouting, and crossed the river. On the other side he found a house with a great bird perched atop it, sleeping. Atli killed the bird with a spear and found Sigrlin and Alof in the house, and took them both back to camp.

They explained that another king named Hroðmar also wanted Sigrlin, and when he was denied her, he invaded, killed Svafnir, and pillaged the land. Then Franmar changed himself into an eagle to keep the girls safe from the invaders. Then Hjorvarð married Sigrlin, and Atli married Alof.

Hjorvarð and Sigrlin had one son, who was strong and handsome, but never spoke, and no name stuck to him. One day, he sat on a barrow, and saw nine valkyries riding, one of whom was the noblest and most beautiful of all of them. She called to him, and said:

7.   "Now Helgi's late to gather rings,
and rule the gleaming fields!
An eagle screams, now you must speak,
or else your heart is weak!"

The man said:

8.   "What comes with such a name, my dear,
since you can offer names?
Think well, for I will not accept
a name without your hand."

She said:

9. "I know a hoard, in Sigarsholm,
   of swords, there's forty-six:
   And one is better than the rest,
   the golden bane of shields.

10. The hilt has rings, the guard has courage,
   there's terror in the blade,
   There's bloody snakes along the edge,
   and adders on the sheath!"

She introduced herself as Svava, daughter of king Eylimi. She was a valkyrie, and rode the air and sea. She named him Helgi, and protected him in battle.

Helgi said:

11. "You may be famous, father, but
   I do not think you're wise!
   You let the flames consume the homes
   of those who caused no harm.

12. Now Hroðmar owns the golden rings
   that mother's father had!
   He rules the spoils of the dead,
   and he'll inherit death!"

Hjorvarð promised to help Helgi, if he wanted to go and avenge Svafnir. So Helgi went with Atli, and they slew Hroðmar, and performed many great deeds. Among these was the slaying of the fiend named Hati, who he found resting on a mountain. After this, Helgi and Atli rested their boats in Hatafjorð. Atli was on watch for the first part of the night. Hrimgerð, Hati's daughter, approached him and said:

13. "What heroes dwell in Hatafjorð?
   Your ships are hung with shields,
   you look as if you don't know fear,
   so say your leader's name."

Atli said:

14.   "His name is Helgi, you will not
hurt him in any way!
Our ships are ringed with iron walls,
we have no fear of fiends!"

Hrimgerð said:

15.   "And who are you, my noble one?
Do you not have a name?
Your lord is trusting, if he lets
you stand and watch the bow."

Atli said:

16.   "I'm Atli, I'll be cruel to you,[63]
for I despise your kind!
I've often stood upon the bow
and given witches death!

17.   Now give your name, you vile beast,
and give your father's name!
You should be far beneath the earth,
with trees above your corpse!"

Hrimgerð said:

18.   "My name is Hrimgerð, Hati's girl,
he was he mightiest.
He won a harem from their homes,
till Helgi cut him down."

Atli said:

19.   "You waited by our ships, you witch,
in ambush by the fjord!
You want to send us down to Ran
if you can't pierce our flesh."

---

[63] There is an untranslatable pun here. Atli's name derives from the adjective *atall* "cruel", so he says something like "I'm Cruel, and I'll be cruel".

Hrimgerð said:

20. "You are delusional, or dreaming,
 your brows replace your eyes!
 My mother ambushed Hloðvarð's sons
 and drowned them in the sea!"

21. You'd neigh if you had any balls,
 for I have raised my tail![64]
 I think your heart is up your ass,
 though you speak like a stag!"

Atli said:

22. "I'd seem a stag, if we would fight,
 if I could go ashore!
 I'd beat you to a pulp, you slut,
 and make you drop your tail!"

Hrimgerð said:

23. "Then come ashore, if you're so tough,
 let's meet in Varin's bay!
 I'll straighten all your twisted ribs,
 if I get hold of you."

Atli said:

24. "I'll come when all the men are up,
 and they can guard my lord.
 I would not be surprised if fiends
 came up from down below."

Hrimgerð said:

25. "Awaken, Helgi, pay me back,
 since you had Hati killed!
 If I can sleep beside you once,
 that will be good enough!"

Helgi said:

26. "A hairy brute's the man for you,
 you nasty, fiendish girl!
 He lives on Þolley, wise but foul,
 I think that he's your type!"

---

[64] A sexual invitation; many animals raise their tails when in heat.

Hrimgerð said:

27.   "I see, you'd rather have the girl
who scanned the sea last night!
She shone like gold, her strength was great,
she shielded all your ships!
It seems because of her I can't
enact revenge on you."

Helgi said:

28.   "Now hear me! I will pay you back
if you will tell me this:
This girl who shielded all my ships,
was she alone or not?"

Hrimgerð said:

29.   "Three groups of nine, but one in front,
bright white and helmeted.
And dew in valleys, hail in peaks
fell from their horses' manes.
They gave mankind a happy harvest,
I hated all of it!"

Atli said:

30.   "Look east, you fool, for Helgi has
assured you'll meet your end!
His ships are safe on land and sea,
his soldiers cannot die!"

Helgi said:

31.   "The day has dawned, and Atli has
delayed you till your death!
A lovely landmark you will make,
for now you've turned to stone!"

Helgi was a mighty warrior indeed. He went to King Eylimi and asked for the hand of his daughter, Svava. They exchanged vows, and loved each other dearly. One year, Helgi went off to war, while Svava stayed home with her father. Heðin stayed in Norway with King Hjorvarð.

That year, on the eve of Yule, Heðin was out for a stroll in the woods when
a troll woman, riding a wolf with a bridle made of snakes, asked him for
sex. He refused her, and she swore he'd pay for this at the oath-cup. That
evening, the boar[65] was brought out, and everyone laid their hands on it,
and swore their oaths by the oath-cup. Heðin drunkenly swore that he
would have Svava, his brother's wife, for himself. The next day, he
regretted it so much that he fled the country, and went into exile in the
south. During his wanderings, he came upon Helgi's camp.

Helgi said:

32. "Welcome, brother! What has brought
   you all the way from Norway?
   What's driven you from father's lands
   to find me here, alone?"

Heðin said:

33. "An evil has befallen me,
   the worst I've ever faced!
   At Yule I swore, in foolish haste,
   that I would have your wife!"

Helgi said:

34. "It's not your fault, for drunken deeds
   we both will suffer soon!
   For Hroðmar's son has summoned me,
   I meet him in three days,
   I think I won't return alive,
   and so it will work out!"

Heðin said:

35. "You told me once that I deserved
   goodwill and gifts from you!
   It's better that you stain your blade
   and not give peace to foes."

---

[65] At Yule, legally binding oaths were sworn upon a sacred boar.

200

Helgi explained that he now suspected his death was due, and that his fetches[66] had appeared to Heðin in the form of the troll-woman on the wolf. Alf, son of Hroðmar, had marked a field in Sigarvell with hazel sticks, and Helgi was to go there in three days' time.

Then Helgi said:

36.   "The troll who tried to sleep with you,
the one who rode at night,
She knew the son of Sigrlin
would fall at Sigarvell."

There was a great fight that day, and Helgi was mortally wounded.

37.   Then Sigar, Helgi's man, went off
to get Eylimi's girl.
He told her to get ready fast
for Helgi soon would die.

Sigar said:

38.   "My lady, Helgi's sent me here,
he wants to see your face
and hear your voice a final time
before his breath is gone."

Svava said:

39.   "What's beaten Helgi, Hjorvarð's son?
What vicious sorrow's come?
If sea or blade has bitten him,
I swear I'll slaughter them!"

Sigar said:

40.   "He fell today at Frekastein,
the best beneath the sun.
Now Alf will have the victory,
though he does not deserve it."

---

[66] Female guiding-spirits, which were believed to appear to their bearer near their appointed time of death.

41.   "Hello, my love! Do not despair,
though we won't meet again,
for blood is flowing under me,
a blade has pierced my heart!

42.   I beg you, Svava, do not weep,
but hear my final words!
Prepare the bed for Heðin now,
and give him all your heart."

Svava said:
43.   "I swore in my beloved home,
when I was given rings,
I would not marry fameless men
when Helgi passed away."

Heðin said:
44.   "Then kiss me, for I won't return
from war to gleaming fields
until the death of Hjorvarð's son
has justly been avenged!"

It's said that Helgi and Svava were reincarnated.

Helgakviða Hundingsbana I

The First Tale of Helgi Hundingsbane

Introduction

Helgakviða Hundingsbana I "The First Poem of Helgi Hundingsbane" appears only in the *Codex Regius*, where it is titled *Vølsungakviða* "The Poem of the Volsungs". It is notable among the Eddic poems for its extensive use of kennings, second only to *Hymiskviða*.

HH I follows another hero named Helgi, who is heavily implied by *Hjørvarðssonar*'s ending to be Helgi, son of Hjorvarð, reborn. Like his namesake, this Helgi falls in love with a valkyrie, implied to be Svava's rebirth, and must defend her from an unwanted arranged marriage.

As previously discussed, the incorporation of Helgi into the Volsung family was likely a later development, so the fact that this poem makes Helgi a Volsung would make it seem that this poem is a late creation. Its frequent use of kennings also implies that its author was quite familiar with skaldic verse. *HH I* also reads much like a praise poem of the sort often written by skalds, devoting much time to highlighting Helgi's bravery and martial skill. These facts all point to the poem being a child of the 11th or early 12th centuries, perhaps composed by a court poet accustomed to writing praise poems for a royal sponsor.

1.   One day, in ancient times, the eagles called
and holy water fell from heaven's heights
when Borghild, Sigmund's wife, in Bralund birthed
the hero Helgi, wise and strong of heart.

2.   The night descended, and the Norns arrived
and shaped the prince's life and deeds to come.
They chose that he would be a mighty king
and would be called the best of Buðli's blood.

3.   With skill immense they wove the threads of fate,
meanwhile, in Bralund, Helgi broke the walls.
They set the golden strands in place for him,
and held them fast within the lunar hall.

4.   They tied the ends upon the east and west,
between them both would Helgi have his land.
Then Nera's sister[67] threw into the north
the final strand, that it would always hold.

5.   A single thing brought pain to Volsung's son,
and to the woman who had birthed his son.
A raven on a branch said to its mate,
in hope of food: "There's something that I know!

6.   The son of Sigmund stands in armored mail
when newly born; at last the day has dawned!
He has a fighter's eyes, he's friend to wolves,
soon raven-kind will have a royal feast!"

7.   His subjects thought he was the son of Day,
and said that happy years were due to come.
And Sigmund came from war to see his son
and gift the noble prince a mighty leek.[68]

---

[67] A Norn. Nera's identity is unknown.
[68] A sword.

8.   He named him Helgi, gave Hringstað[69] to him,
       Solfjoll, Snaefjoll, Sigarvell as well,
       Hringstoð, Hatun, lastly, Himinvang;
       Sinfjotli's brother got a bloody snake.[70]

9.   And so, amidst his friends, he grew up strong
       a noble elm in shining light of joy.
       He gladly gave his soldiers gleaming gold,
       his bloody hoards were shared with everyone.

10.   The boy could not wait long to go to war,
       he'd only made it fifteen years before
       he slaughtered mighty Hunding, who had ruled
       for many years a kingdom vast and strong.

11.   The sons of Hunding asked from Sigmund's son
       a hoard of wealth, for golden rings and gems.
       Their honor asked that they be paid in kind
       for Helgi's plundering and Hunding's death.

12.   But Helgi swore he'd give them not a thing,
       for Hunding's death there'd be no bounty paid.
       He said instead he'd gladly pay them back
       with storms of ashen spears and Oðin's wrath.

13.   Their armies gathered on the battlefield,
       near flaming peaks, the place they'd settled on.
       The peace of Froði tore apart that day,
       while Viðrir's hungry hounds[71] surrounded them.

14.   And Helgi did not rest until he'd killed
       both Alf and Eyjolf by the eagle-stone,
       and also Hunding's sons, Havarð and Hjorvarð,
       he butchered that entire dynasty.

---

[69] Probably modern Ringsted, Denmark.
[70] A sword.
[71] Wolves. Viðrir is a name of Oðin.

15.   A ray of light erupted from the peaks,
         then lightning flashed and danced across the sky,
         and armored women came from heaven's field,
         their coats of mail were flecked with crimson blood,
         their spears emitted beams of golden light.

16.   The son of Day called out from deep within
         the woods, as all the southern ladies passed,
         if they would celebrate the victory
         and travel home with all the warriors.

17.   Then Hogni's daughter sprang from off her horse,
         the soldiers' laughter stilled, and she declared:
         "We have another task we must fulfill,
         and so we cannot stay and drink with you.

18.   My father's promised me to Granmar's son,
         and claims he is a brave and noble man,
         his name is Hoðbrodd, but I think he is
         about as brave as kittens chasing string!

19.   And soon he'll come to claim me as his wife,
         I need a man to face him on the field
         or steal me far away from Hoðbrodd's grip."

20.   "Don't be afraid of Isung's killer, girl!
         While I'm alive, you won't be claimed by him!"

21.   The lord of all sent runners far and wide,
         through air and sea, for sailors and for swords.
         He offered each a glowing hill of gold
         to anyone who'd go to war with him."

22.   "They must go quickly to the ships," he said,
         "and then in haste from Brandey we must go!"
         And long he waited there, until at last
         a host of heroes came from Heðinsey.

23.   And then from Stafnsnes the ships were launched,
       their golden hulls were gliding over waves,
       then Helgi turned to Hjorleif, and he asked,
       "Have you examined those who follow us?"

24.   Then Helgi turned and shouted to his men,
       "We're slow to count the ships of Tronueyr,
       those dragon-headed steeds all stuffed with men
       which now are sailing into Orvasund!"

25.   "There's fourteen-forty loyal men with us,
       our foes in Hatun wait with double that,
       I think we've got a roaring day ahead!"

26.   The captain dropped the tents from off the mast,
       so all the noble soldiers would arise
       and see the brow of Day[72] ignite the east.
       The sails were lifted, and the ships were off
       from Varinsfjorð, to war and valiance.

27.   The oars were shrieking, and the iron clanked,
       and shields were smitten as the vikings rowed.
       The prince's fleet went surging far from land,
       each ship was filled with battle-hungry men.

28.   The ocean thundered, and their keels grew long
       as Kolga's sisters[73] lashed their sides with force
       enough to smash the cliffs or break the sea!

29.   But Helgi had the sails drawn higher still,
       his sailors did not fear the vicious waves
       though Aegir's daughters tried with all their might
       to send the ocean-horses to the depths.

30.   And mighty Sigrun, brave as any man,
       ensured their ships would stay afloat.
       At last the floating beasts could wrench themselves
       from out of Ran's embrace at Gnipalund.

---

[72] The rising sun.
[73] Waves. *Kolga* is a daughter of the sea-god Aegir, whose name is often used to refer to waves.

31.   When night descended over Unavag,
the golden fleet of Helgi met the shore.
On Svarin's mound his foes were watching them,
with heavy hearts they scanned the hostile ships.

32.   Then Guðmund asked, the prince of noble blood:
"Who leads a hostile army to my coast
and guides his horrid hordes to beach themselves?"

33.   Sinfjotli shouted back, and raised his shield
above the yard, its golden rim agleam.
He was the best of them at smithing words,
indeed, the best at insult-trades with lords!

34.   "Announce tonight, while you are feeding pigs
and luring bitches to the trough of swill,
the Ylfing clan have come from eastern lands
through Gnipalund, with battle on our minds!

35.   This is the place where Hoðbrodd will meet Helgi,
the prince who fears to flee, amidst the ships.
He's given eagles many times a feast
while you were making out with milling slaves!"

36.   "It seems you do not know the ancient tales
when you fling falsehoods at your betters, boy!
I know you've feasted on the guts of wolves
and that you've slaughtered half your family!
Your mouth is cold, you've drained the wounds of men,
and slither in the stones, for no one loves you!"

37.   "I saw you working spells in Varinsey,
you spun your lies, as women tend to do!
You said you wanted no one in your bed
except for me, of all the warriors!

38.   Another time you were a valkyrie,
a mighty, lovely girl in Oðin's hall!
His champions were fighting over you,
you two-faced girl, I bet you liked it too!"

39.   "Have you forgotten that we sired cubs?
           But I was not the one who birthed them, bitch!"

40.   "You surely did not father Fenrir's cubs,
           although your age exceeds the wolf's by years!
           You couldn't have, because in Gnipalund
           some fiendish ladies cut your nutsack off!"

41.   "I've heard you had to sleep beneath the hay,
           for you were used to sleeping with the wolves!
           And every sort of evil followed you
           when you ripped holes into your brothers' chests!
           You're only famous from the worst of deeds!

42.   But then in Bravoll you were Grani's bride,
           with golden bridles, eager for the ride!
           I rode you far, down many hills, until
           your energy was spent, and down you fell!"

43.   "It seemed you had no sense of decency
           when you were milking goats for Gullnir, prick!
           I know that you were Imðr's daughter once,
           and dressed in rags; have I yet told enough?

44.   I'd sooner feed your corpse at Frekastein
           to ravens, ravenous for blood and flesh,
           than lure your bitches to the swill, or feed
           your balless boars; may devils eat you whole!"

45.   Then Helgi said, "Sinfjotli, it is best
           for us to fight and give the eagles food,
           instead of hurling empty words around,
           regardless of the hate we feel for them.

46.   Though Granmar's sons are hardly good to me,
           a noble man should always speak the truth.
           Our enemies displayed at Moinsheim
           that they are skilled enough at wielding blades."

47.   Then from the coast did Guðmund's men depart
        and fled to Solheim on their speedy steeds,
        through dewy dales and hilltops veiled in shade,
        the sea of mist would tremble where they passed.

48.   They met with Hoðbrodd by the courtyard's gate
        and warned him that a foe was on the way.
        His eyes, encased in helmet, scanned the host
        and how they rode, and then he proudly called,
        "The Niflungs' faces are all filled with fear!"

49.   "Their nimble ships are turning toward the shore,
        their yards are long and strong as steel," said Guðmund,
        "They're lined with many shields and shaven oars,
        and each is full of vicious Ylfing men.

50.   There's fifteen companies now approaching land,
        and seven thousand more in Sogn wait.
        They're lying off the coast of Gnipalund,
        their ships are black and blue, and lined with gold.
        But that's the bulk of all the men they brought,
        I fear that Helgi won't delay for long!

51.   Send runners to our allies far and wide,
        to Sparin's lands we ought to send a man,
        and send a pair beyond the murky woods!
        Do not let any soldier lag behind
        who's skilled enough to fight with wounding flames![74]

52.   We'll need both Hogni and the sons of Hring,
        Atli, Yngvi, and also Alf the Old,
        they're always happy on the battlefield,
        we will not shy away from Volsung's boys!"

53.   As fast as passing glances, battle came
        and gleaming weapons clashed at Frekastein.
        And at the front was Helgi, Hunding's bane,
        who always was the first to join the fight,
        for war to him was ecstasy, he feared
        to flee, and had a heart as hard as stone!

[74] Swords.

54.   Then armored ladies came from high above
        and shielded Helgi as the fight grew fierce.
        Then Sigrun said, as wounding women came
        and devils' horses ate from Hugin's feast:[75]

55.   "All hail to Sigmund's son and Yngvi's kin,
        you'll have both love and joy for all your days,
        For you have slain a fearless foe today,
        who brought the death of many frightful men!

56.   My noble prince, you've more than shown yourself
        deserving both of treasure and of me!
        In victory, my love, you will enjoy
        the lands of Hringstað, Hogni's daughter, too,
        and fame and praise, for now the battle's done!"

---

[75] "Devil-horses" are wolves. "Hugin's feast" is corpses.

Helgakviða Hundingsbana II

The Second Tale of Helgi Hundingsbane

Introduction

Helgakviða Hundingsbana II "The Second Poem of Helgi Hundingsbane" is also only found in the *Codex Regius*, titled *Frá Vølsungum* "About the Volsungs". Its composition style is much like that of *Hjǫrvarðssonar*, consisting of scattered poetic verses linked together with prose.

HH II overlaps a great deal with *HH I*, covering many of the same events as that poem, but also deals with the aftermath of Helgi's victory, and his fatal mismanagement of his defeated enemies.

HH II is, even more obviously than *Hjǫrvarðssonar*, a fusion of verse fragments bound by prose. This is all but stated by the prose regularly attributing the poem's verses to other, older poems. Notably, stanza 19 quotes a close variant of a stanza from *HH I*, and calls it *Helgakviða* "Helgi's Poem". This means that *HH II* must have been complied after *HH I*, possibly in the late 11th or 12th century, though as with *Hjǫrvarðssonar*, the poems it cites must be older than that.

King Sigmund, son of Volsung, married Borghild of Bralund. They named their son Helgi, after Helgi, son of Hjorvarð. He was fostered by Hagall.

There was also a mighty king named Hunding, for whom Hundland was named. He once went raiding with his many sons.

There was a lot of hostility between Sigmund and Hunding, and they killed each other's kin. Sigmund's clan was called both Volsung and Ylfing. Helgi scouted Hunding's lands in disguise. Heming, son of Hunding, was there. As Helgi was going to depart, he met a shepherd on the way and said to him:

> 1.   "Go tell your lord that Helgi knows
> the armored man he killed!
> A wolf has come into his house,
> who Hunding thought was Hamall!"

Hamall was the son of Hagall. Hunding sent men to Hagall's lands to find Helgi. Helgi could only save himself by dressing as a slave girl and working the mill. Hunding's men looked for Helgi, but could not find him, until the evil Blind spoke up and said:

> 2.   "What hateful eyes that woman has,
> she is no kin of slaves!
> She rends the very stones themselves,
> the mill is straining too!

> 3.   A prince has earned a nasty fate,
> for now he mills the grain!
> It seems her hand should hold a sword
> and not a twisting stone!"

> Hagall answered him and said:
> 4.   "A roaring mill means nothing, see,
> for she's no simple slave.
> For once she rode above the clouds
> and fought as vikings do,
> but Helgi took her as his own,
> for she's of royal blood,
> that's why her eyes are flame!"

218

Then Helgi fled and went to his ships. He killed Hunding and was thus called Helgi Hundingsbane. He camped with his army in Brunavag, and there they slaughtered stolen cattle, and ate the flesh raw.

There was a king named Hogni, and he had a daughter named Sigrun. She was Svava reborn, and like her was a valkyrie, riding air and sea. Sigrun rode to Helgi's ships and said:

5. "Who leads the fleet that's floating here?
Where did you travel from?
What do you need in Brunavag?
Where are you heading to?"

Helgi said:
6. "The ships we have are Hamall's fleet,
from Hlesey have we come.
In Brunavag we wait for wind,
we're heading to the east!"

Sigrun said:
7. "Where did you waken battle, prince,
and feed my sisters' birds?[76]
Why is your armor splashed with blood,
why is your beef uncooked?"

Helgi said:
8. "From western lands we've just returned,
we Ylfings battled there.
I captured bears in Bragalund
and fed the birds with spears.

9. And that's the reason why I'm here,
and why my beef is raw."

Sigrun said:
10. "You speak of war! How Hunding fell
before the might of Helgi!
For kinsmen's deaths you were avenged,
your blade was damp with blood."

---

[76] Ravens. Sigrun is a valkyrie, so her sisters are also valkyries.

Helgi said:

11. "My lady, how can you be sure
 that we've avenged our kin?
 There's many noble fighters here
 and they could be my kin."

Sigrun said:

12. "I wasn't far away from you
 when Hunding sank and died,
 and sly, I think, is Sigmund's son,
 in tales of slaughter-runes!

13. I saw you on the ships as well,
 before the bloody bow
 and lashed with icy waves.
 The son of Day thinks he's unknown,
 but Hogni's girl knows him!"

There was a king named Granmarr who ruled over Svarinshaug. He had three sons: Hoðbrodd, Guðmund, and Starkað. Hoðbrodd went to a meeting of kings, and he gained the hand of Sigrun, Hogni's daughter. When she was informed of this, she took her valkyries and flew over the sky and sea to find Helgi.

Helgi was by a volcano, where he had killed Alf, Eyjolf, Hjorvarð and Hervarð, the sons of Hunding. Helgi was tired after this, and was resting beneath the eagle-stone when Sigrun came to him, embraced and kissed him, and told him of her plight, as is described in the old *Tale of the Volsungs*:[77]

14. So Sigrun sought the happy prince,
 and took his hand in hers.
 She hugged his helm and kissed the prince,
 and then his heart was warmed.

15. She said from when she saw his face
 she fell for Sigmund's son.

---

[77] A lost poem.

16.   "To Hoðbrodd I have been betrothed,
but I want you instead.
But now I fear my family's wrath
for breaking Father's wish!"

17.   The girl spoke true to how she thought,
she wanted Helgi's hand.

Helgi said:

18.   "Don't fear your father's wrath, my love,
or family's evil thoughts!
Come live with me, I'll keep you safe
for I don't fear your kin!"

Helgi then gathered a fleet and sailed to Frekastein. On the way, they met a brutal storm that threatened to sink them. They looked up and saw flashing lighting, and rays of light shining on the ships. Nine valkyries were riding above them, with Sigrun at the head. Then the storm passed and they sailed to land.

Granmar's sons were sitting on a hill when they saw the ships approaching. Guðmund got on his horse and scouted the fleet on a cliff by the harbor. By that point, the Volsungs had already lowered their sails. Then, as is written in the *Tale of Helgi*,[78] Guðmund called out:

19.   "Who leads an army to my coast
and guides them to the beach?"

20.   What Skjolding leads these ships to war?
I see your golden flags,
I think you haven't come in peace,
your flags cast viking-rage."

---

[78] Likely *HH I*, though the quoted stanza is slightly different from that poem.

Sinfjotli, son of Sigmund, answered him, which is also written:

21. [79] "Let Hoðbrodd know that Helgi's come,
the one who fears to flee!
He'll bind your homelands to himself
and all your gold is his!"

Guðmund said:

22. "I think instead at Frekastein
we will 'discuss' our woes!
For Hoðbrodd's vengeance soon will come
if long we are oppressed!"

Sinfjotli said:

23. "I think you'd rather tend the goats
and flee atop the cliffs
and hold a hazel staff in hand
than stand in Brimir's court!"

Helgi said:

24. "For you, Sinfjotli, it is best
to fight and feed the birds
than fling our foes our empty words
regardless if we hate them!

25. Though Granmar's sons are hardly good,
we still must speak the truth.
For they displayed at Moinsheim
that they can wield a sword
and that they're brave indeed!"

Then Guðmund rode home with news of the invaders. Granmarr's sons then raised an army led by many kings, including Sigrun's father, Hogni, and her brothers, Bragi and Dag. There was a great battle, in which the Volsungs won and killed all the royals there, except Dag, who swore oaths of fealty to them. Sigrun searched among the slain and found Hoðbrodd on the brink of death. She said to him:

---

[79] In the manuscript, this flyting occurs after the battle scene. I have moved it here for logic's sake.

26.   "Now Sigrun, born of Sevafjoll,
        won't flop into your arms!
        The lives of Granmarr's sons have passed
        and devils' steeds consume them!"

Then she found Helgi and was overjoyed. He said:

27.   "Your luck has not been perfect, love,
        the Norns have caused you grief.
        Your father and your brother fell
        to me at Frekastein.
28.   And then at Styrkleif Starkað died,
        at Hlebjorg, Hrollaug's sons.
        His body fought without its head,
        I've never seen its like.

29.   Your kin are scattered all around
        and all of them are dead.
        You're fated to cause strife immense
        between the strongest men."

Sigrun wept.

                    Helgi said:
30.   Take comfort, love, you've been our shield,
        we can't escape our fates!"

                    Sigrun said:
31.   "I'd wish that they could live again
        and still we could embrace!"

Helgi married Sigrun, and they had sons, while Helgi was still young.
Dag, Hogni's last son, sacrificed to Oðin for vengeance for his father's
death. Oðin responded by giving Dag his spear.

Dag lured Helgi out to Fjotrlund, then ran him through with the spear and
killed him. Then Dag went home and told Sigrun the news. He said:

32.   "My sister, grief I hate to bring,
your tears are not my wish.
This morning fell at Fjotrlund
the best beneath the sun,
who stood on soldier's necks."

Sigrun said:

33.   "May all the oaths you swore to him
come back and bite your ass!
By all the shining streams of Leipt
and frigid stones of Unn![80]

34.   May ships not sail beneath your feet
despite a helpful wind!
May steeds not run beneath your legs
if foes are rushing you!

35.   May blades grow blunt when you're around,
unless they strike your neck!
Then I'll get justice for his death
if you must live like wolves,
deprived of wealth and pleasant things
and food, except the dead!"

Dag said:

36.   "You're mad, you've fully lost your mind,
to curse your brother so!
For Oðin is the source of ills,
he cast the runes of strife!

37.   I'll give you rings of reddest gold,
and Vandilsve and Vigdal,
Take half our lands for all the harm
I've caused you and your boys!"

---

[80] Both a pair of mythological rivers.

Sigrun said:

38.   "I'll have no joy in Sevafjoll,
        by day and not by night,
        if light won't shine on Helgi's band
        and Vigblaer runs beneath him,
        and I can greet my love!

39.   My love inspired fear intense
        in foes and in their kin
        like wolves create in nanny-goats
        that makes them flee the peaks!

40.   My Helgi grew above mankind
        as ash surpasses thorns,
        and like the fawn that's drenched in dew
        but grows above the rest,
        whose antlers light the sky!"

A barrow was made for Helgi. When he went to Valhalla, Oðin invited him to rule alongside him.

Helgi said:

41.   "It will be Hunding who will wash
        our feet and light the hearths!
        He'll feed the horses, leash the dogs,
        and feed the pigs at night!"

Sigrun's maid was out for a walk one night when she saw Helgi's ghost ride to his barrow with an army.

She said:

42.   "Is this a trick, or has perhaps
        the end of days arrived?
        The dead are riding, spurred by spears,
        the kings are heading home!"

Helgi said:

43.   "There is no trick, your eyes are true,
        the gods have not yet died.
        the valiant dead have not returned,
        I've traveled here myself."

The maid went home and said to Sigrun:

44.   "The barrow's opened, Helgi's come,
go out and see your man!
His wounds are bleeding, needing staunched,
he wants that you should come!"

Sigrun went into Helgi's barrow and said to him:

45.   "I am as pleased to see you here
as Oðin's greedy hawks[81]
when, drenched with dew, they see the dawn
or smell a slaughtered corpse!

46.   I want to kiss your bloody bones
before you drop your coat!
Your hair is stained with hoary frost,
your corpse with slaughter-dew,[82]
your hands are cold as lashing rain!
How can I heal you, love?"

Helgi said:

47.   "Because of you, Sigrun, my love,
am I now sopping wet.
Your golden face is drenched with tears
each night before you sleep.
They fall as blood upon my chest
with swollen, searing grief.

48.   Let's drink tonight a happy drink,
though I've lost love and land!
Let's not sing mournful songs tonight,
despite my mortal wounds!
Now brides are buried here with us,
the wives of valiant men!"

---

[81] Ravens.
[82] Blood.

Sigrun made a bed in the barrow.

49.   "I've made a bed in here for us,
my Helgi, Ylfing-born.
Please hold me in your arms tonight
as if you were alive!"

Helgi said:

50.   "I say that anything may come
to me at morn or eve,
when in my rotting arms you sleep,
a beauty in the mound,
as if we both were still alive,
my Sigrun, born of kings.

51.   It's time to take the ruddy road
that leads to heaven's heights.
I must be west of mortal lands
before Salgofnir[83] crows!"

Then Helgi and his men rode away, and the women went home. The next night, Sigrun had her maid watch the barrow. At sunset, Sigrun went to the barrow and said:

52.   "If he was coming, he'd be here,
my love from Oðin's hall.
My hopes to see him now have passed,
for eagles sit on ash
and soldiers sink to sleep."

The maid said:

53.   "Don't go alone to dead men's homes,
my lady, keep your mind!
For revenants have strength at night
they lack when day is bright!"

---

[83] Presumably Valhalla's rooster.

Sigrun died of grief shortly after this. In ancient times, people believed
that the dead were reborn, but we know now that this is nonsense. It is said
that Helgi was reborn as Helgi Haddingjaskaði, and that Sigrun was
reborn as the valkyrie Kara, daughter of Halfdan, as is told in *Kara's
Song*.[84]

---

[84] This poem is lost, and the story of Helgi and Kara is thus unknown.

228

Frá dauða Sinfjǫtla

The Death of Sinfjotli

Introduction

Frá dauða Sinfjøtla "About Sinfjotli's Death" is a short prose story that links the *Regius*'s three Helgi poems with its lengthy series of Sigurð poems.

It summarizes the story of Sigmund's life after the death of Helgi Hundingsbane, notably the death of his eldest son Sinfjotli and fathering of the hero Sigurð. Though it may be based on older poems now lost, the version of events here is likely the work of either the *Regius* author or the author of whatever manuscript the *Regius* is based on. It is thus almost certainly a 13th- century work.

Sigmund, son of Volsung, was the king of France. He had three sons: Sinfjotli, Helgi, and Hamund. His wife, Borghild, had a brother named ???.[85] Sinfjotli and ??? both wanted to marry the same woman, and Sinfjotli killed ??? over it.

When he came home, Borghild wanted him outlawed, but Sigmund offered her compensation, and she had to accept it. But, at the funeral feast, Borghild took a hornful of poison and put it in Sinfjotli's beer. When Sinfjotli looked at his drink, he saw the poison in it, and he said to Sigmund, "Father, my drink is cloudy." Then Sigmund drank Sinfjotli's beer, as his superior constitution made him immune to poison, but his sons were only immune to poison on the skin; if they drank any, they would surely die. Borghild brought him a second drink, and things went as before. She then brought him a third drink, and called him a pussy if he refused to drink it. Sinfjotli told Sigmund of this, and he said, "Try filtering it through your beard, son!" Sinfjotli did this and died immediately.

Sigmund carried his corpse a long way, until he reached a fjord. He saw a boat there, with an old man in it. He offered to bring Sigmund across, but when he put Sinfjotli's body in the boat, the man said the boat was full, and he would have to go around the fjord by land. Then the old man and the boat vanished into thin air.

Sigmund stayed in Denmark, in Borghild's lands, for a long time. Then he went back to his own land in France. There he married Hjordis, daughter of King Eylimi. They had one son, whose name was Sigurð. Sigmund eventually was killed in battle by Hunding's sons, and Hjordis married Alf, son of King Hjalprek of Denmark, which is where Sigurð grew up.

Sigmund and his sons were stronger and braver than other men, and they performed the most famous deeds. Sigurð was the greatest of all of them, and in the old stories he was known to be the most immaculate of men and the most valorous of warriors.

---

[85] There are gaps in the text where the name should be, and the *Volsunga Saga* never refers to the man by name.

Grípisspá

Gripir's Prophecy

Introduction

Grípisspá "Gripir's Prophecy" is preserved in the *Codex Regius* manuscript, and begins its series of poems about the life and death of the mortal hero Sigurð. It serves as a summary of the events of Sigurð's life, narrated by his uncle Gripir, who is apparently known for his prophetic skills.

This poem begins the *Regius*'s series of Niflung poems, the Norse adaptation of tales that likely originated in Germany. This can be seen in the fact that the setting and place names are entirely located in that area, as well as the fact that many of the poems' characters seem to be based on historical figures from continental Europe. They follow the rise and fall of the hero Sigurð and of the Niflungs, the Burgundian royal family who Sigurð marries into.

As it is a summary of stories that would have been well-known when they were circulating orally, *Grípisspá* is likely no older than the first books containing these poems. It is thus likely dates from the 12th or 13th century.

Gripir, son of Eylim, was Hjordis's brother. He ruled lands, and of all
humankind he was the wisest and most far-sighted. Sigurð, riding alone,
once came to Gripir's hall. He was easily recognized, and met a man
named Geitir outside the hall. Sigurð approached this man and questioned
him, saying:

1.   "Who dwells within the fortress here?
Who is the liege of local thanes?"

2.   "My lord is Gripir, he's the one
who rules the land and all its thanes."

3.   "And is the noble king at home?
May I go in and speak with him?
A stranger's here, advice he seeks,
it's Gripir that I've come to see!"

4.   "My lord and liege will want to know
the name of one who's come to speak with him."

5.   "My name is Sigurð, Sigmund's son,
his only son of Hjordis born."

6.   Then Geitir went inside and said
"A stranger has arrived my lord,
of noble birth he seems to be,
he says he's come to meet with you."

7.   So Gripir went outside and said
"Come in, my boy, you're welcome here,
you're never late or early here!
Now, Geitir, go and tend his horse!"

8.   Then long they spoke of many things,
in just the way that wise men do,
"Now tell me, uncle," Sigurð said,
"what can you tell me of my fate?"

9.   "You'll be the best beneath the sun,
the highest born of humankind,
be free with gold, but fear to flee,
with handsome looks and wisest words!"

10.   "Now tell me more, I wish to know,
        if you can see so far ahead,
        what benefits will come to me
        when I depart your hall and lands?"

11.   "You'll first avenge your father's death
        and that of Eylimi as well,
        you'll gain a mighty victory
        and butcher Hunding's hardy sons!"

12.   Now tell me, uncle, noble king,
        since we are speaking honestly;
        What famous deeds will I perform
        that will be known at heaven's edge?"

13.   "Alone you'll slay the shining snake,
        the greedy beast of Gnitaheið!
        Both Fafnir's bane and Regin's doom
        you will become; I speak the truth!"

14.   "Much wealth I'll gain, if you are right
        and I accomplish such a feat.
        Now further look, and tell me more,
        what fate awaits me after that?"

15.   "You'll find the dragon's treasure hoard
        and take the gleaming gold as yours.
        On Grani's back you'll load the gold
        and ride away to Gjuki's hall."

16.   "You must continue sharing words,
        my noble uncle, tell me more!
        When I'm a guest in Gjuki's hall
        what fate awaits me after that?"

17.   "Upon a mountain's slept a girl
        since Helgi's death, in glowing mail,
        you'll strike her coat with Fafnir's bane,
        that blade will pierce her metal jail."

18.   "The mail will break, the girl will speak
when she is free from endless sleep.
What will she say to Sigurð then
that lets me gain a joyful life?"

19.   "She'll teach you runes and wisdom, boy,
the things that men of wit should know,
the knowledge of the tongues of men
and how to live a healthy life!"

20.   "So when that's done, the secrets learned,
and it is time to ride away,
now strain your sight, so I can know,
what fate awaits me after that?"

21.   "You'll travel next to Heimir's hall
and gladly be the chieftain's guest.
But that is all that I can see,
it's best you seek no further sight."

22.   "Your lying words have caused me grief,
I think you're seeing further still!
My fate, it seems, is full of pain,
that's why you feign a lack of sight!"

23.   "Your youth was lit the brightest, boy,
and that was what I saw the best.
I'm hardly wise, or far of sight,
there's little more that I can tell!"

24.   "There are no men above the earth
who see as far as you, my lord!
Don't hide the ugly truth from me,
I want to know the harm that comes!"

25.   "You will not have a shameful fate,
take solace in this simple truth!
Your name will live forevermore
as long as humankind endures."

26.   "It would be shameful most of all
        for us to part with truth concealed.
        Though fate is fixed, I want to know,
        my mother's brother, tell it all!"

27.   "Then I will tell you all your fate,
        for you insist so stubbornly!
        And you will see I never lie
        the day your death arrives."

28.   "I do not want your wrath, my lord,
        I simply want your good advice.
        If good or bad, I want to know
        the fate that lies before my hands."

29.   "At Heimir's you will find a girl,
        his foster-daughter, Brynhild called.
        She's Buðli's daughter, but he's raised
        her well, to be a fearless girl."

30.   "So what if she is beautiful?
        What harm will Heimir's girl inflict?
        Now tell me Gripir, everything,
        since you can see the fates of all!"

31.   "The gorgeous girl that Heimir raised
        will take the joys of life from you.
        You will not sleep, or wisely think,
        or speak to men, until you see her!"

32.   "And will I heal my aching heart?
        If you can see, then tell me so!
        Will I the woman's dowry pay,
        and will that lovely girl be mine?"

33.   "The two of you will pledge yourselves
        as bride and groom, but break the oaths.
        When you're a guest in Gjuki's hall,
        your memory of her will fade."

34.   "What's this? Explain this treachery!
        Will I become a fickle man,
        since I will break the oaths I swore
        to her I thought I loved the most?"

35.   "You'll be deceived by someone else,
        for Grimhild's counsels you will suffer.
        Instead her daughter will be yours,
        she'll scheme to lash your line to hers!"

36.   "So Guðrun then will be my bride
        and Gunnar I will have for kin?
        It seems I would be married well,
        if not for guilt for treachery."

37.   "Your mind will bend to Grimhild's plots;
        she'll have you ask for Brynhild's hand
        for Gunnar, lord of all the Goths,
        and you will do the things she wants!"

38.   "I have a vicious fate in hand,
        and all my wisdom will collapse
        If I must give the girl I love
        in marriage-bond to someone else."

39.   "You will swear oaths of loyalty,
        the trio, Gunnar, Hogni, Sigurð.
        You'll swap your shapes while traveling,
        will you and Gunnar, I have seen!"

40.   "What would compel the two of us
        to swap our shapes while traveling?
        I fear deception, worst of all,
        will come; but Gripir, speak the truth!"

41.   "You'll keep your mind, but have his face,
        and yes, you will work trickery!
        You'll win the hand of Heimir's girl,
        and you won't see the harm of it!"

42.   "The worst, to me, is such a deed
       will see my noble name besmirched!
       I'd never trick a girl like that
       and surely not the best of brides!"

43.   "And now I see that you will sleep
       beside her as you would your mom!
       For that alone, your name will live
       As long as humankind endures!"

44.   "Will Gunnar have a noble wife
       among mankind? I want to know!
       Although three nights I slept with her,
       for that there is no precedent!"

45.   "You'll toast your weddings both at once,
       in Gjuki's hall, as brothers bound.
       When you arrive, you'll change your forms,
       but you'll think differently about it!"

46.   "Will marriage therefore lead to bliss
       between us? Gripir, tell me now!
       Will Gunnar live a happy life
       or will the joy be mine alone?"

47.   "You will recall your oaths, but won't
       say anything regarding them.
       Your woman will be glad, but his
       will not, and she will seek revenge!"

48.   "What could I ever offer her
       as recompense for such a ruse?
       She had the oaths I swore to her
       and did not keep; her rage is right."

49.   "She'll say to Gunnar that you lied
       and did not keep the oaths you swore
       when he put all his faith and trust
       in you to win his bride for him."

50. "Then tell me, Gripir, what will come,
    Will I be cursed, as stories say?
    Or will that famous woman lie
    about the things we've done? Say more!"

51. "In rage and grief she will inflict
    on you the greatest harm she can!
    Though you deceived the prince's wife,
    you never will defile her."

52. "But will the brothers of my wife
    respond to Brynhild's vengeful speech?
    Will Gjuki's children stain their swords
    against their sister's man? Say more!"

53. "Then Guðrun's heart grows cold and dark
    when both her brothers cause your death,
    and so, when Grimhild's work is done,
    her girl will know no happiness.

54. Take solace in a single fact
    and know one thing about your fate:
    No man of greater worth than you
    will ever live beneath the sun!"

55. "Let's part as friends, for fate is fixed,
    and I've heard all I came to hear!
    I know you'd say good things about
    my life, if they were meant to be!"

Fáfniskviða

Fafnir and the Treasure Hoard

Introduction

Fáfniskviða "Embracer's Poem" is a name I have invented for this poem, which goes untitled in the *Codex Regius*. The *Regius* presents this poem, along with *Sigrdrífumál*, as a single poem, which was split by 17th-century writers into three: *Reginsmál*, which tells of the backstories of Regin and Fafnir, *Fáfnismál*, which recounts Sigurð's killing of Fafnir, and *Sigrdrifumál*, about Sigurð's freeing of the imprisoned valkyire Sigrdrifa. Though the *Regius* gives no indication that these three were viewed as separate poems, there is a clear transition point between the material dealing with Fafnir and Sigrdrifa, so I have chosen to split *Sigrdrífumál* off, while keeping *Fáfniskviða* united. The cutoff point between the former two "poems" is arbitrary, and the *Reginsmál* section is very disjointed narratively, functioning much better as an introduction to the broader story of Sigurð and Fafnir, so I have chosen to keep them as one story.

Fáfniskviða has likely come down to us in less-than-pristine condition; its verses, much like those of the Helgi poems, are woven in with prose passages, and its use of meter is inconsistent. At the very least, this suggests extensive textual alteration, or, again like the Helgi poems, that verses from several poetic traditions were inelegantly mashed together. Whatever the case, many of these verses are likely quite old; multiple stanzas have *reið* alliterating with *v*-initial words, suggesting a pre-11th century date (see *Lokasenna*'s introduction for a more thorough explanation).

Sigurð went to Hjalprek's stable and picked out a horse for himself, who he named Grani. Then Regin, son of Hreiðmar, came to Hjalprek's land. He was dwarf-sized, but more gifted than any other man. He was wise, stern, and skilled at magic.

Regin fostered Sigurð, educated him, and loved him dearly. He told Sigurð of his ancestors, and of a time when Oðin, Honir, and Loki came to Andvari's waterfall, which had many fish. This waterfall was home to a dwarf named Andvari, who lived there in the form of a pike, and he ate plentifully there.

"We had a brother named Otr", Regin explained, "who often went to the falls in the form of an otter. He caught himself a salmon, and was eating it on the riverbank when Loki beat him to death with a stone. The gods thought they had been lucky, and skinned the otter.

That night, they came as guests to our house, and showed off their kill. We captured them then, and demanded compensation; enough gold to fill the otter-skin, and coat the outside. The gods sent Loki to gather this gold. He got Ran's net from her, then went to Andvari's falls and threw the net out, and caught the pike.

Then Loki said:

1. "What foolish fish is swimming here
    but cannot guard itself?
    Now free your head from Hel's embrace,
    and get the water's flame!"[86]

The fish said:

2. "My name's Andvari, Oin's son,
    I've gone through many falls.
    The Norns arranged it long ago
    that I should live in streams."

3. Then Loki said, "Now tell me, dwarf,
    if you would keep your life:
    How does mankind resolve disputes
    if wounding words are flung?"

---

[86] Gold.

4.   "A hefty price is paid by those
who wade in Vaðgelmir.[87]
For men who trade in lying words
the punishments are long!"

Then Loki saw that Andvari had a massive hoard of gold, and demanded Andvari give it to him. He did so, but tried to keep one ring, which Loki refused to let him keep. The dwarf went into the stone and said:

5.   "The golden hoard that Gust once owned
will end two brothers' lives
and cause eight noblemen distress!
May none enjoy the gold!"

The gods then gave Hreiðmar the gold, filling the otter-skin and standing it up on its feet. Hreiðmar inspected the skin and found one whisker exposed, and told them to cover it. Oðin then brought out the ring Andvaranaut and covered it.

6.   Then Loki said, "The gold is yours,
my head has brought you wealth.
Your sons will gain no joy from it,
it will destroy you both!"

Hreiðmar said:
7.   "You gave us gifts, but not your sorrows,
and not with all your hearts!
I would have bled the life from you
if trickery I feared."

Loki said:
8.   "And I foresee the worst will come,
for kin will slaughter kin!
The warriors this curse will strike
are not yet even born!"

---

[87] possibly the river of punishment mentioned in *Vǫluspá*.

Hreiðmar said:

9. "For all my days I think I'll rule
  and be a wealthy man!
  Your threats provoke no fear in me,
  go back the way you came!"

Then Regin and Fafnir, his other brother, asked for compensation from Hreiðmar for Otr's death, but he refused them. That night, Fafnir ran his father through with a sword while he was sleeping. As he lay dying, Hreiðmar called to his daughters and said:

10. "Lyngheið and Lofnheið,
  my life has gone away,
  and now I need avenged!"

Lyngheið answered:

11. "No sister dares avenge her dad
  by butchering her kin!"

12. "Then may you bear a daughter, wolf,
  and not a noble's son,
  and have her wed a desperate man
  so he'll avenge your pain!"

Then Hreiðmar died, and Fafnir took all the gold for himself. Regin asked him for a share, but Fafnir only gave him a "no". Then Regin went to Lyngheið, his sister, for advice on how to get a share. She said:

13. "With loving-kindness ask the man
  again to claim your share.
  Inheritance should not be claimed
  from kin at point of sword!"

Regin told Sigurð about all these things. One day, Sigurð went to Regin's house, and was warmly welcomed. Regin said:

14. "The son of Sigmund has arrived,
  the hero to my hall!
  His strength exceeds my aging might,
  he'll be like leashing wolves!

15.   I will instruct the valiant prince,
        for Yngvi's kin is here!
        He'll be the best beneath the sun,
        and famed throughout the lands!"

Sigurð and Regin were inseparable after that, and Regin told him that
Fafnir was living in Gnitaheið in the form of a massive snake. He had a
fear-helm, which terrified all living beings.

Regin made Sigurð a sword named Gram. He dipped the sword in the
Rhine, and dropped a bit of wool in the current, and the sword cut through
the wool the same as the water. Sigurð used it to cut Regin's anvil in half,
and after that Regin encouraged Sigurð to go and kill Fafnir, but Sigurð
said:

16.   "Eylimi's hair will never gray,
        and those who made it so
        will laugh if I pursue a hoard
        without avenging him!"

Hjalprek gave Sigurð a fleet, so he could avenge his father and
grandfather. They hit a storm, and headed for shore. A man was standing
on a cliff and called out:

17.   "Who's riding high on Raevil's horse[88]
        upon the raging sea?
        Your ocean-steeds are lashed with sweat,
        the wind will fell them soon!"

                Regin answered:
18.   "I'm here with Sigurð on the ships,
        to death we're led by breeze!
        The decks are smashed, our ships are shaking,
        who calls and asks these things?"

19.   "Since Hugin loved young Volsung's kills,
        by Hnikar I've been known.
        The mountain man, the Gripper, Wise
        I'm called; I need a ship!"

---

[88] A kenning for a ship.

They sailed to land, and let the man on their ship, and the weather calmed
immediately.

Sigurð said:

20. "Now tell me, Hnikar, if you know
   the fates of gods and men,
   if one must fight and swing his sword,
   what omens are the best?"

Hnikar said:

21. "There's many signs that men should know
   when they go swing their swords.
   A raven's an auspicious sight
   for sword-trees[89] on the road.

22. I know another; if you're out
   and ready for the road.
   If you see waiting on your porch
   two men who lust for fame.

23. I know a third; if you should hear
   a wolf beneath the ash,
   you'll have good fortune in the fight
   if you should see them first.

24. Don't ever fight if you can see
   the sister of the moon!
   He'll have the win, the one who sees,
   or forms an army-snout.

25. If you should fall before a fight,
   that is an awful sign!
   It means there's women at your side
   who want to do you harm.

26. Well-combed and fed it's good to be,
   and fed at morning-time.
   You don't know where you'll be at night,
   do not ignore the signs."

---

[89] Warriors.

Sigurð fought a great battle against Lyngva, Hunding's son, and his brothers. All of them were killed, and afterwards Regin said:

> 27.   "A bloody eagle has been carved
> upon the bane of Sigmund!
> Here Sigurð fought the best of all,
> and he's made Hugin glad!"

Then Sigurð returned to Hjalprek's lands, and Regin encouraged him to go kill Fafnir.

Sigurð and Regin went to Gnitaheið, and there they found the track that Fafnir made as he slithered to the water. Sigurð dug a big hole, and hid inside it. As Fafnir slithered away from his gold, he spewed poison, which rained down on Sigurð's head. When Fafnir passed over the hole, Sigurð sprang up and stabbed Fafnir through the heart with his sword. The serpent writhed and lashed out with his head and tail. Then Sigurð climbed out of the hole, and met the snake's eyes.

> Fafnir said:
> 28.   "You, boy of boys,[90] who sired you?
> What boy has fathered you?
> Whose blade was reddened with my blood,
> whose sword has pierced by heart?"

Sigurð hid his name, for in those days it was believed that a man's dying curse could be vicious if he cursed his foe by name.

> He said:
> 29.   "I'm called a noble beast, you see,
> I've come here motherless!
> I was not fathered like mankind,
> I always walk alone."

> Fafnir said:
> 30.   "Then tell me how you came to be
> without a father, boy!"

---

[90] The manuscript reads "boy and boy"; this translation is essentially a guess.

Sigurð said:

31.   "You do not know my family,
I tell you, nor do I!
My name is Sigurð, Sigmund's son,
my blade has pierced your heart!"

Fafnir said:

32.   "Now tell me who incited you
to come destroy my life!
You had a bitter father, boy,
a magpie he has raised."[91]

Sigurð said:

33.   "I was incited by my will,
and aided by my blade!
No man who's brave when he is old
was cowardly in youth."

Fafnir said:

34.   "If you were raised among your friends,
I'd see you fight with rage.
But now you're bound, in war enslaved,
and captives always shake!"

Sigurð said:

35.   "You fling your insults, for I'm far
from where my father lived.
I've not been bound, in war or peace,
you'll find my will is free!"

Fafnir said:

36.   "You just hear hatred in my words,
but know I speak the truth;
that gleaming hoard of screaming gold
will lead you to your death!"

---

[91] The text of this line in the manuscript reads "inborn magpie on a spoon"; the translation here is speculative.

Sigurð said:

37.   "Well, someone has to guard the gold
until that day arrives.
A time's prescribed when every man
must travel on to hell."

Fafnir said:

38.   "The Norns have set it soon for you,
for fools do not live long!
For doomed men all is dangerous,
you'll drown against the wind."

Sigurð said:

39.   "Then tell me, Fafnir, if you're wise
and know so many things,
who are the Norns who come at birth
and draw the children out?"

Fafnir said:

40.   "The Norns have many families,
they're not one single race,
for some are gods, and some are elves,
and some are Dvalin's girls."[92]

Sigurð said:

41.   "Then tell me, Fafnir, if you're wise
and know so many things,
what is the island called where Surt
will battle with the gods?"

Fafnir said:

42.   "Its name is Oskopnir, the place
where gods will play with spears.
The Bilrost breaks behind their steeds
and they will wade the stream.

43.   My helm of fear once frightened men
while I laid over gold!
I thought I was the best of all,
it seems I've met too few!"

---

[92] Dwarves.

Sigurð said:

44. “A helm of fear won't keep you safe
  when wrathful ones arrive.
  A traveler will often find
  they're not the best of all!”

Fafnir said:

45. “I once breathed poison when I laid
  upon my father's hoard.”

Sigurð said:

46. “Your hissing was intense indeed,
  your heart was hard as well,
  but hatred grows in humankind
  for him who has the helm.”

Fafnir said:

47. “Young Sigurð, hear my wise advice,
  for it will serve you well.
  Ride home, and leave the hoard behind,
  the gold will be your death!”

Sigurð said:

48. “You've said your piece, but I must go,
  for I've a hoard to claim!
  I'll leave you in the throes of death
  where Hel may have you, snake!”

Fafnir said:

49. “My brother is a snake as well,
  he's led us both to death!
  My life is fading quickly now,
  your might is more than mine.”

Regin had left while Sigurð was fighting Fafnir, and came back just as
Sigurð was cleaning his sword.

Regin said:

50. “Young Sigurð's gained the victory
  and Fafnir lies a corpse!
  Of all the men who walk the earth,
  you are the boldest yet!”

254

Sigurð said:

51.   "It's hard to tell when humans clash
who is the bravest born.
The blades of many valiant men
are never stained with blood."

Regin said:

52.   "You're happy for your victory
while drying Gram on grass.
It's true you slew my brother, but
I had a part as well."

Sigurð said:

53.   "You goaded me to ride across
the holy mountains here.
The snake would still have life and wealth
if you'd not called me out."

Then Regin cut out Fafnir's heart with his sword, Riðil, and drank some
blood from the cut.

Regin said:

54.   "Keep watch, my boy, for I must sleep,
while you roast Fafnir's heart!
I want to eat my brother's heart
and slurp up all his blood."

Sigurð said:

55.   "You ran away while I made red
my blade in Fafnir's heart!
I fought the snake with all my might
while you hid in the brush!"

Regin said:

56.   "The ancient devil would have stayed
much longer in the grass
without the blade I made for you
to wield against the snake!"

Sigurð said:

57.   "But courage beats the sharpest swords
    when wrathful beings clash,
    the brave can get the victory
    despite a blunted blade.

58.   The brave are better than the weak
    when clash of battle comes.
    The joyous more than the depressed
    can face the tides of fate."

Then Sigurð cooked Fafnir's heart on a spit. When it was fully cooked, blood began foaming out of the heart, and Sigurð dipped his finger to taste it. He burnt his finger, and in a panic, licked it. When the blood touched his tongue, he gained the ability to understand birds. He heard finches chirping in the trees above him, and they said:

59.   "And there sits Sigurð, splashed with blood
    and roasting Fafnir's heart!
    He'd prove his wisdom if he ate
    the shining slice of life!"

60.   "And there lies Regin, scheming plots
    to trick the trusting boy!
    In rage he weaves a web of lies
    to punish Fafnir's bane!"

61.   "The elder should be shorter by a head
    when he arrives in hell!
    Then Sigurð may command the gold
    that Fafnir sat above."

62.   "He would be wise if he would take
    your wise advice, my sisters!
    He would do well to gladden Hugin,
    for ears reveal a wolf!"[93]

---

[93] An idiom akin to *where there's smoke, there's fire.*

63.   "The battle-tree would be a fool,
        more so than he should be,
        if he keeps Fafnir's age away,
        but lets his brother flee!"

64.   "Indeed, he'd be unwise to let
        the army-slicer live!
        There Regin lies, the traitor sleeps,
        and can't protect himself!"

65.   "That devil should be shorter by a head
        and far from all the gold,
        so then the gold that Fafnir had
        will be the boy's alone!"

                    Sigurð said:
66.   "I think his fate won't be so great
        that he'll announce my death,
        for he will join his brother soon
        along the road to hell!"

Sigurð cut off Regin's head, and then ate Fafnir's heart and drank the
blood of the two brothers. After that, he heard the finches singing, and
they said:

67.   "Now, Sigurð, bind the golden rings,
        for kings have little fear!
        I know a woman flush with gold,
        and loveliest of all.

68.   Take verdant roads to Gjuki's hall,
        your fate will lead the way!
        He's raised a worthy daughter there,
        and you will buy her, boy!"

69.   "I know a hall in Hindarfjall
        with flame around its edge.
        it was constructed by the wise
        from Ogn's shining light.[94]

---

[94] Probably gold.

70.   A battle-lady's sleeping there,
with linden's bane[95] above.
Ygg did not want the men she slew,
and so he pierced her side."

71.   But you can see beneath her helm,
young man of Skjoldung blood,
you won't break Sigrdrifa's sleep
before the Norns' decree!"

Then Sigurð rode along Fafnir's track to his lair, and found the door open. It was made of iron, as was the door-frame and all the supports, which were dug into the earth. Inside he found a massive hoard of gold, and filled two chests with it. He also took the fear-helm, a golden hauberk, and the sword Hrotti and many more treasures, and loaded Grani with them. But the horse would go nowhere without Sigurð on his back.

---

[95] Fire.

Sigrdrífumál

The Wisdom of Sigrdrifa

Introduction

Sigrdrífumál "Victory-Driver's Words" is found untitled in the *Codex Regius*, appended to *Fáfniskviða* with no indication of being a separate entity. 17th-century writers copying the *Regius* split it off into a separate poem and gave it its modern title.

It tells of Sigurð's rescue of the imprisoned valkyrie Sigrdrifa, who according to a note in the margins of the *Regius* is the same person as Brynhild, the valkyrie who goes on to give Sigurð so much trouble. The *Volsunga Saga* also conflates the two, though it is an open question whether they were always the same or not.

The poem's ending is missing from the *Regius*; a total of eight pages are missing from the book at this point, which has consumed both this poem's ending as well as the bulk of *Sigurðarkviða*. Thankfully, the 17th-century writers have preserved the poem's ending, whether from the *Regius* before the loss or another, now lost, manuscript.

Sigurð rode up to Hindarfjall and southward to France. On the peak he saw a great light, as if a massive fire were burning, shining across the sky. When he climbed to the top he saw a wall of shields, with a banner on top. Sigurð went inside and found someone sleeping, fully armed. He removed the helmet and saw that she was a woman. Her chainmail was stuck tight to her, as if it had melded into her flesh. He drew Gram and cut the mail from top to bottom, and along the sleeves. Then he pulled the hauberk off the woman. As soon as it came off, she woke up and said:

1. "Who cut the coat? How have I woke?
   Who broke the pallid chains?"

        He answered:
2. "My name is Sigurð, Sigmund's son,
   I cut the raven-snacks."[96]

3. "My dreams were endless, long I slept,
   and long are humans' pains.
   For Oðin cast a sleeping spell
   that I could not ignore."

Sigurð sat her down and asked her name. She filled a horn with mead and gave him a memory-drink.

4. "I greet the Day and all his sons,
   and Night and all her kin!
   Look down on us with wrathless eyes
   and grant us victory!

5. I greet the gods and goddesses
   and Earth, the bountiful!
   Grant us wisdom, eloquence,
   and healing hands for life!"

---

[96] Chainmail. This likely refers to the ravens having to dig around the mail on a corpse to get to the flesh beneath.

She gave her name, Sigrdrifa, and said she was a valkyrie. She told Sigurð what had happened to her. There had been two kings fighting a war. The first, Hjalm-Gunnar, was an old man, but a distinguished warrior, and Oðin had promised him victory. The other was Agnar, brother of Hoða, who no one would receive. Sigrdrifa killed Hjalm-Gunnar, and Oðin, enraged by this, pierced her with a sleep-thorn and said she would take a husband. She objected, for she had sworn an oath that she would only marry a man who could not feel fear.

Sigurð then asked her to teach him the wisdom of all the worlds.

Sigrdrifa said:

6.   "I bring you beer, young tree of war,[97]
that's mixed with strength and fame.
It's filled with songs and helpful staves,
with spells and runes of joy!

7.   The runes of victory are good
if you would win in war.
On hilt and blade and sheath they go
and twice you must name Tyr.[98]

8.   The runes of beer are good to know
to keep your trysts unknown.
On horn and hand they should be carved
and ᚾ[99] upon the nail.

9.   To ward off evil, bless a cup,
and put a leek inside.
I know your mead will never be
mixed up with evil things.

10.   Protection-runes are good to know
if children must be born.
On palms and joints they should be carved,
then ask the disir's aid.

---

[97] Once again, a warrior. Humans are often referred to poetically as trees.

[98] This may refer to a verbal invocation, or perhaps writing the rune ᛏ, also called *Tyr*.

[99] Called *nauðr*, "constraint", presumably to bind the woman's will so she won't reveal the affair.

11.   The runes of sea are good to know
to keep your ships afloat.
They go on stem and rudder blade
and burned into the oars.
The raging waves won't break so high
that you will not be safe.

12.   The runes of limbs are good to know
to cure the wounds of men.
They should be carved on bark of trees
whose branches face the east.

13.   The runes of speech are good to know
to ward revenge away.
You have to wind and weave them well
and set them all the same
at Things, where men from all around
resolve their great disputes.

14.   The runes of mind are good to know
to be the wisest man,
for they were read and they were carved
when Oðin brought them up,
they leaked from skull of Heiðdraupnir
and horns of Hoddrofnir.

15.   He stood on peaks with Brimir's edge,[100]
a helm upon his head,
then Mimir's head awoke and spoke
the first and wisest words.

16.   They're on the shining lady's shield,
and wheels of Rungnir's car,
on Arvak's ear and Alsvið's hoof,
on Sleipnir's teeth and sled-chains,

---

[100] A sword.

17.   on Bragi's tongue and paws
        of bears, on claws of wolves,
        on eagles' beaks and bloody wings,
        and on the footing of a bridge,
        on midwives' palms and servants' prints.

18.   on glass and gold and amulets,
        in wine and wort and thrones,
        on Gungnir's tip[101] and Grani's chest,
        upon nails of Norns
        and on the beaks of owls.

19.   The runes he carved were shaven off,
        and mixed with holy mead,
        and sent across the realms.
        The gods have some, the elves have some,
        the Vanir have some more,
        and humans have the rest.

20.   The runes of beech and runes of guard
        and all the runes of beer
        and mighty runes of strength
        are free for anyone to use
        if he can learn them well
        until the gods' demise!

21.   And now, young maple-armory,
        there is a choice to make!
        Choose speech or silence, but recall,
        all evil is ordained."

              Sigurð said:
22.   "I will not flee if I am doomed,
        I was not born afraid!
        I want to know your wise advice
        as long as I'm alive."

---

[101] Oðin's spear, which always hits its target.

Sigrdrifa said:

23. "Then first I say that to your kin
you should be free of fault.
Don't take revenge if they give cause,
that serves a dead man well.

24. I tell you next, don't swear an oath
that you cannot uphold.
Bad oaths invite a bitter fate,
for cursed are wolves of words!

25. I tell you third, do not dispute
with men who lack a brain,
for fools will often scatter words
more evil than they know.

26. Do not be silent, for it seems
that quiet men are weak.
A noble name is hard to keep
unless it's justly earned,
so end his breath another day,
and show his words are false!

27. I tell you fourth, if evil ones
are waiting on the road,
keep traveling, don't be their guest,
though night may swallow you.

28. A warrior needs sharpened eyes
when he goes off to fight,
but evil women stalk the roads
to blunt their blades and brains.

29. I tell you fifth, if you should see
a girl who's beautiful,
don't let her dowry rule your dreams
or lure her in for love!

30.   I tell you sixth, if drunken words[102]
        grow cruel beyond compare,
        do not dispute with battle-trees,
        for wine will steal your wits.

31.   For songs and beer have often caused
        great sorrow for mankind,
        they've come from death and evil spells,
        the many pains of men.

32.   I tell you seventh, if you sue
        a man who's brave in war,
        to fight is always better than
        a burning in your home.

33.   I tell you eighth, to shun the bad,
        avoid deceitful spells.
        Don't play around with women, boy,
        or falsely pleasure them!

34.   I tell you ninth, protect the dead,
        wherever they may lie.
        Those slain by sickness or by sea
        or by a weapon's edge.

35.   Prepare a bath for those who've died,
        and wash their hands and head,
        then bury them when combed and clean,
        and pray they rest in peace.

36.   I tell you tenth, don't ever trust
        the vows of bandits' sons,
        least not the ones whose dads you've slain
        or caused their brothers' deaths!
        A wolf may lie in living sons,
        despite the joys of gold.

---

[102] After this point, eight pages are missing from the *Regius*. The rest of this poem comes from seventeenth-century paper manuscripts.

37.   For gold will not make hatred sleep,
        nor pain and sorrow die.
        A prince will need his wits and weapons
        if he will be the best.

38.   I tell you last, protect yourself
        from evil while you live.
        I think your life will not be long,
        for mighty conflict comes!"

Sigurðarkviða

The Fall of Sigurð

Introduction

As previously mentioned, the *Codex Regius* is missing eight pages, beginning part-way through *Sigrdrífumál*. This can be seen even in scans of the manuscript; there is notable damage to the binding at this point. The page on the other side of this gap contains 19 stanzas of what appears to be a poem that began on the missing pages.

Unlike *Sigrdrífumál*, there are no paper copies of this poem; the missing sections are lost, probably forever. However, the missing events are summarized in both the *Prose Edda* and the *Volsunga Saga*. The latter quotes four otherwise unknown stanzas of poetry, which almost certainly were found on the missing pages.

Sigurðarkviða's original length has been disputed. The missing pages contain enough space for around 200 stanzas of poetry. It is possible that there are multiple missing poems on those pages, but there is good reason to suspect that most, if not all, of these stanzas belong to *Sigurðarkviða*. The poem the *Regius* calls *Sigurðarkviða in skamma* "The Short Version of Sigurð's Poem" clocks in at 71 stanzas, among the longest Eddic poems. If that is the "short" version, it calls into question how long the "long" version is.

This poem's unusual situation requires a different approach to presenting it. I have summarized the missing events in prose English, with the four stanzas from the *Volsunga Saga* mixed in, then resumed the usual poetic rendering once the story reaches the sections that survive in the *Regius*.

After sharing her wisdom, Sigrdrifa told him her mortal name: Brynhild, daughter of Buðli, king of the Huns. She and Sigurð professed their love for each other, and swore oaths to one day marry each other and no one else.

After parting ways with Brynhild, Sigurð traveled to Burgundy, where he was received as an honored guest by Gjuki, king of the Burgundians. There Sigurð was introduced to Gjuki's two sons, Gunnar and Hogni, and his beautiful daughter, Guðrun. Gjuki's wife, Grimhild, was a powerful witch, and she knew of Sigurð's famous exploits as well as the enormous hoard of gold he had taken from Fafnir, and wanted him to marry her daughter. She also knew of his love for Brynhild, and so she gave Sigurð a potion that caused him to forget about her. She then convinced Gjuki to offer Guðrun's hand to Sigurð in marriage, which he quickly accepted. He, Gunnar, and Hogni all swore oaths of loyalty and friendship to each other, and Sigurð spent a year there with his new family.

After that, Grimhild suggested to Gunnar that he should go and marry Brynhild. He and Sigurð traveled east, to the Huns' lands, and asked her father Buðli for Brynhild's hand. The king agreed, but warned them that Brynhild had hidden herself in a castle surrounded by fire, and had sworn she would only marry a man who was brave enough to cross it. Gunnar tried to do so himself, but was not brave enough to go through the fire. He and Sigurð then used a spell Grimhild had taught them to change bodies, and Sigurð, now in Gunnar's body, mounted Grani and braved the flames:

1.   The flame was raging, earth itself was rocked,
the rising fire surged to heaven's heights.
Few men had lived with courage strong enough
to ride or leap across the burning wall.

2.   But Sigurð's blade made Grani gallop forth,
at his approach the fires dimmed and died.
They fell before the glory-greedy prince,
and lit the flashing armor Regin made.

Then Sigurð went into the castle, and slept beside Brynhild for three nights, placing his sword between them so they could not touch each other. After the third night, they exchanged rings and swore they would marry. Sigurð then returned with good news, and gave Gunnar his body back.

Gunnar and Sigurð then married Brynhild and Guðrun, respectively, in a joint ceremony, and had happy marriages for a few years. Sigurð and Guðrun had two children together: a daughter, Svanhild, and a son, Sigmund. Then, one day, Brynhild and Guðrun were bathing together in the Rhine, and Brynhild said that she and Guðrun should not share the same bathwater, because her husband was far nobler than Guðrun's. Guðrun protested, citing Sigurð's killing of Fafnir and claiming his hoard, but Brynhild countered by saying that Gunnar had ridden through the flames around her castle, where Sigurð could not. Incensed, Guðrun told Brynhild the truth about Sigurð's deception, and showed her the ring she had given "Gunnar", which Sigurð had given her. Brynhild angrily swore revenge, saying:

> 3.   "For Sigurð slew the snake, and all mankind
>   will tell that story while the world endures!
>   It seems your brother was not brave enough
>   to ride or leap across the burning wall."

Brynhild fell ill after this, and Gunnar came to visit her. She flew into a rage at the sight of him, hurling vicious insults and threatening his life. Gunnar and Hogni had to chain her to keep her from ending him right then and there, and she screamed so loud that she could be heard throughout all the lands.

Gunnar and Hogni both tried to speak with her, but she refused to see either of them. Eventually, at Guðrun's urging, Sigurð went to see her, but she became even angrier at his appearance. She cursed him, and said she regretted that she could not stain her sword red with his blood. Sigurð said back that he had regained his memory of the oaths they'd sworn, that he still loved her, and offered to leave Guðrun for her. Brynhild angrily refused him, swearing she didn't want him or any other man. At that, Sigurð had no choice but to depart:

> 4.   As Sigurð left their fruitless talk behind,
>   the loyal friend of princes bowed his head.
>   Regret then filled the valiant hero's heart,
>   his coat of iron split along the sides.

Gunnar tried to speak to Brynhild again after Sigurð left, but she refused to have anything to do with him until he killed Sigurð. She also told him the reason she was so upset was because Sigurð had taken her virginity when he was in Gunnar's body. Gunnar then summoned Hogni to him, and they hatched a plan:

Hogni said:

5.   "(My brother, what has Sigurð)[103] done to you
        that's made you want to see his life destroyed?"

Gunnar said:

6.   "He gave me honeyed oaths, but all were false,
        he swore, then broke, a vow of loyalty!
        They say that Sigurð's true to all his oaths,
        and yet he tricked me in the worst of ways!"

Hogni said:

7.   "It seems that Brynhild's crafted evil here
        and lit your rage to cause you vicious harm!
        I think she holds a grudge for Guðrun's love
        and hates that you'll enjoy her all your days!"

8.   They killed a wolf and snake, and roasted them,
        and Guthorm got the greedy creatures' meat,
        before the brothers, keen to see him dead,
        could lay their hands upon the gallant man.

9.   They slew him in the south, beyond the Rhine,
        and in the branches' heights a raven crowed:
        "Your blood will stain the edge of Atli's blade!
        As you betrayed, so will you be betrayed!"

10.   Outside was waiting Guðrun, Gjuki's girl,
        and called at once when all the men arrived:
        "I see my brothers riding in the front,
        what fate has found my Sigurð, lord of men?"

11.   And only Hogni dared to answer her:
        "We cut your man to pieces with our swords,
        and Grani hangs his head above his corpse."

---

[103] The first half of this line is on a missing page. This is a common scholarly suggestion.

12.   Then Brynhild, Buðli's daughter, called to him:
"And now the land and weapons will be yours!
I know that Sigurð would have ruled them all
if he had clung to life a while more!

13.   I think it's hardly right for him to rule
the wealth of Gjuki and a host of men,
Five sons does Gjuki have, but Sigurð none
to lead his armies, and who thirst for war!"

14.   Then Brynhild laughed, a single roaring boom,
with all her heart, and made the hall resound,
"And now the land and weapons will be yours,
because you led the hero to his doom!"

15.   Then Guðrun, Gjuki's daughter, yelled aloud:
"What wounding words I've had to hear from you!
May Gunnar, Sigurð's slayer, fall to fiends,
I swear, I'll see your hateful deeds avenged!"

16.   The night grew dark, the beer had all been drunk,
and all their pleasant words had been exchanged.
They went to bed, and soundly fell asleep,
except for Gunnar, who was wide awake.

17.   He shook his feet, and mumbled to himself,
his mind was clouded by his fearful thoughts.
The eagle's words[104] resounded in his mind,
the raven's speech was keeping him from sleep.

18.   Then Brynhild, Buðli's daughter, snapped awake,
the princess rose before the break of dawn,
"The harm's been done, no matter what you think,
I'll speak my grief, or else I'll die in pain!"

19.   The room fell still at Brynhild's wrathful words,
beyond all knowledge are a woman's thoughts,
when, weeping, she began to speak about
what, laughing, she had made her husband do.

---

[104] Presumbly a stanza is missing in which an eagle also prophesies Gunnar's death.

20.   "I dreamed a dream quite dark and dreary here,
        the hall was frozen, and my bed was cold,
        I saw you riding with a joyless heart,
        with limbs all chained, surrounded by your foes.

21.   And I have seen that all the Niflungs' kin
        will lose their might, for you are wolves of word!

22.   So fast you have forgotten, Gunnar dear,
        when you and Sigurð bled into your prints!
        You've paid his loyalty with evil deeds,
        though he was always foremost in the fight.

23.   He showed his faithfulness the day he came
        as you, to see me and request my hand.
        The bane of armies always kept the oaths
        he swore to you; I kept my maidenhood!

24.   He placed a wounding wand between us both,
        a gilded blade, its edges forged in flame
        and carved with poison drops, at both our sides,
        three days and nights, while he was in my bed!"

This poem says that Sigurð was killed outside in the woods, just as
German people say. But other stories say he was killed in bed, and *The
Old Tale of Guðrun* says that he was killed while heading to a Thing. But
they all say this in unison: Sigurð was deceived and ambushed while he
was lying down and unprepared to defend himself.

Guðrúnarkviða I

Guðrun's Lament

Introduction

Guðrúnarkviða "Guðrun's Poem" is the first of several laments contained in the *Codex Regius*. The poem details Guðrun's grief for the murder of Sigurð, progressing from stunned silence to open weeping to finally being able to eulogize her husband.

This poem has some similarities in both style and phrasing to *Guðrúnarkviða II*, which suggests that one of these two may have drawn from the other. The latter poem is likely among the Edda's oldest, and the description of Guðrun's mourning of Sigurð is unique to this poem, suggesting it may be a Norse innovation. With this in mind, it is likely that this poem is younger than *Guðrúnarkviða II*, perhaps making it a work of the late 10th or 11th century.

When Sigurð died, Guðrun sat over his corpse. She did not cry like other women, but was about to explode from grief. Men and women alike both went to comfort her, but that was no easy task. Some say that Guðrun had eaten some of Fafnir's heart and could understand the speech of birds. This was also written about her:

1.   In early days, when Guðrun longed for death
and grieved unceasingly by Sigurð's corpse,
she did not wail or clasp her hands in grief
or mourn her man the way that women should.

2.   Then nobles, wide in wisdom, came to her
and tried in vain to break her grim façade,
but Guðrun, in her grief, could scarcely weep,
if she could feel, her heart would burst apart.

3.   And then the wives of all the lords arrived,
in gold bejeweled, and seeking Guðrun's side,
And each told Guðrun of their greatest pains,
the sorrows most severe they'd ever had.

4.   The first to speak was Gjaflaug, Guðrun's aunt:
"I am the girl most loveless on this earth!
Five husbands I have had, and five I've lost,
eleven siblings and two daughters, too,
and even still I've carried on alone!"

5.   But Guðrun could not shed a single tear,
such was her anguish at her husband's loss
and hardened was her heart before his corpse.

6.   Then Herborg, queen of all the Huns, declared:
"Then hear of even greater grief I've faced!
My seven sons were slain in southern lands
in valiant battle, and my husband too!

7.   My father, mother, and my brothers four
were used as playthings by the wind and waves,
the raging sea destroyed their wall of boards.

8.   And none but I could dress and bury them,
        or make them ready for the trip to hell!
        A single season brought me all of that,
        no living person brought me any joy.

9.   Then I was bound, a prisoner of war,
        the very season that my family died!
        I had to gild and bind the shoes that went
        upon the feet of some ungrateful queen.

10.   In jealousy, she vented rage at me
        and beat me constantly with heavy blows!
        I've never known a better lord in all
        my days, or known a woman worse!"

11.   But Guðrun could not shed a single tear,
        such was her anguish at her husband's loss
        and hardened was her heart before his corpse.

12.   The next to speak was Gullrond, Gjuki's girl:
        "Your wisdom, Herborg, has not shown you how
        to offer comfort to a grieving wife!"
        She ordered Sigurð be exposed to air.

13.   She pulled the shroud from off of Sigurð's face
        and cushioned it upon her sister's lap,
        "Now look at him, and put your lips on his
        the way you did when he was drawing breath!"

14.   A single moment Guðrun looked at him.
        She saw his hair, stained brown and soaked with blood,
        his glassy eyes that once were lit with life,
        and where the sword had split his heart's defense.

15.   Then Guðrun slumped, and sank into the shroud,
        her hair came loose, her face went flaming red,
        a single drop of rain descended to her knees.

16.   Then Guðrun, Gjuki's daughter, wept at last,
        the stream of tears flowed through her golden locks,
        and in the yard her geese all honked as one,
        the noble birds that Guðrun long had owned.

16.   Then Gullrond, Gjuki's daughter, said to her:
       "I know the love you shared went far beyond
       what anyone on earth has ever known.
       You had no joy, no matter where you were,
       without your Sigurð standing by your side!"

17.   "My Sigurð towered over all my kin
       as spears of garlic loom above the grass.
       He was the brightest stone upon the band,
       a gleaming rock upon a prince's hand!

18.   To all the soldiers of the king I seemed
       a higher sight than all of Herjan's girls![105]
       But now I'm smaller than a willow-leaf
       without my Sigurð standing by my side!

19.   I miss him in my throne and in my bed,
       my friend in speech; and I know who's at fault!
       For Gjuki's sons have caused my suffering
       and made their sister weep with tortured tears!

20.   Your lands will be as empty as the oaths
       you swore to Sigurð long ago!
       I swear that Gunnar will not gain the gold
       and Sigurð's hoard will lead you to your doom,
       and everyone's who swore the broken oaths.

21.   There was no greater joy in Gjuki's lands
       than when my Sigurð mounted Grani's back
       and went to get for Gunnar Brynhild's hand,
       what evil luck that vile woman brought!"

22.   Then Brynhild, Buðli's daughter, answered her:
       "May she forever lack a man and kids,
       the one who drew this weeping out of you
       and used the runes of speech to make you speak!"

---

[105] Valkyries. This might be a subtle swipe at Brynhild, herself a valkyrie.

23.   Then Gullrond, Gjuki's daughter, shouted back:
        "Shut up, you evil hag, you've said enough!
        You've always been the doom of noble men!
        You're driven on by spite and evil fates,
        you've been the greatest pain for seven kings,
        and left too many women lacking love!"

24.   Then Brynhild, Buðli's daughter, answered her:
        "My brother, Atli, is the cause of this!
        For Buðli's son you should reserve your hate!

25.   When we were living in the Hunnish halls,
        we saw that Sigurð had the serpent's light.[106]
        I've paid immensely for that single trip,
        and I regret I ever saw the sight!"

26.   And then she rose and summoned all her strength,
        the eyes of Buðli's daughter burned with flame!
        She saw the wounds that littered Sigurð's corpse,
        and snorted poison at the sight of them.

Guðrun fled into the woods, and went all the way to Denmark, and spent three and a half years with Þora, Hakon's daughter.

Brynhild could not bear to live without Sigurð. She killed eight slaves and five maids, then stabbed herself, as it says in *The Short Version of Sigurð's Tale*.

---

[106] Gold.

Brynhildarkviða

Brynhild's Wrath

Introduction

This poem is referred to both as *Sigurðarkviða in skamma* "The Short Version of Sigurð's Poem" and *Kviða Sigurðar* "Sigurð's Poem" in the *Codex Regius*. These names are humorously ironic, as Sigurð barely features in it, and the poem is in no way short; at 71 stanzas, it is among the longest in this book, a fact which brings into question how long *Sigurðarkviða* must have been if its "short" version is so long. Its most prominent character is not Sigurð but Brynhild, and so I have given it the name *Brynhildarkviða* "Brynhild's Poem".

The poem's primary subject is Brynhild's bloody revenge against Sigurð for his deception of her, covered only briefly in *Sigurðarkviða*. Unlike previous poems, which tend to condemn Brynhild's vengeance as too extreme, this poem almost justifies it, with Brynhild heavily emphasizing the wrongs done to her by the Niflungs and Sigurð.

Brynhild's final prophecy suggests that the poet who composed this poem was familiar with the rest of the Niflung stories, suggesting this poem is probably a later composition. If it was originally intended as an abbreviation of *Sigurðarkviða*, then it obviously must postdate that poem as well. The 12th century seems a fairly safe bet.

1.	In early days, king Gjuki had a guest:
	the dragon-slayer, born of Volsung's blood!
	Young Sigurð got the oaths of both his sons,
	the heroes all swore oaths of loyalty.

2.	He got a girl, and wealth beyond compare,
	he wed young Guðrun, Gjuki's gorgeous spawn,
	They drank and fought together many days,
	inseparable were Gjuki's sons and Sigurð.

3.	Until they went to ask for Brynhild's hand,
	and Sigurð rode to get her for his friend,
	for Volsung's grandson knew the way to her,
	he would have had her, if he'd had his mind.

4.	The southern hero laid a naked sword,
	a rippling blade, between them in her bed.
	He did not place his lips on Brynhild's flesh,
	nor did he hold her body in his arms,
	instead, he kept her pure for Gunnar's bed.

5.	She'd known no wrongs or injury or death
	for all the days she'd walked upon the earth,
	She'd never known disgrace, or dreamed of such,
	but soon her fate would show her all of these.

6.	She sat outside, alone, at day's decline
	and there she said aloud, to open air,
	"I must have Sigurð, or I swear he'll die,
	for either way I'll hold him in my arms!

7.	Tomorrow I'll regret the things I've said,
	but he has Guðrun, and Gunnar is my man,
	the Norns have given us a painful fate!"

8.	She'd often go outside, her evil heart
	as cold as glaciers, as the stars came out.
	While Guðrun went to join her man in bed
	and Sigurð wrapped the sheets around his wife
	so he could hold her close and keep her warm.

9.   "I have no joy, I have no man I love,
        my only comfort is my rotten heart!"

10.   She spoke herself into a frenzied rage,
        "I'll see that Gunnar loses everything,
        he'll have no lands, he surely won't have me,
        a prince can hardly make me satisfied!

11.   I will return to lands from whence I came
        and never leave my family again!
        And there I'll stay and sleep my years away,
        unless he draws the hero to his death
        and show that he's a better man than him!

12.   His son must also share his father's fate!
        A little wolf must not survive for long!
        Without a son to carry on his name,
        a bitter pill will vengeance prove to be."

13.   When Gunnar heard, his heart grew deathly ill,
        he bowed his head and sifted through his thoughts.
        He sat like that until the west grew dark
        but did not know what his desire was
        or tell what virtue would demand of him,
        for Sigurð's heart was very close to his,
        the Volsung's loss would rob all joy from him.

14.   He weighed his options till the east was bright,
        it was unheard of in the first of days
        for queens to up and leave their kings alone,
        and so he summoned Hogni to his side,
        in every way was he a faithful friend.

15.   "To me, my Brynhild is a perfect wife,
        there is no better love than Buðli's girl!
        I'd sooner lose my life than for a day
        the love and wealth of someone such as her.

16.   We must betray our friend and gain his gold,
        and then control the metal of the Rhine!
        We'll live in peace, and meet our every need
        and savor all the juice of fortune's fruits."

17.   In answer, Hogni said a single thing:
"No man of honor would do such a thing,
not cut apart the oaths we swore to him,
or end a friendship at the point of spears.

18.   There are no men more happy in the world
than those commanded by the four of us
while Baldr of the armies still draws breath.
No marriage-brotherhood exceeds our own,
not even that of all the sons we'll have
and rear to be the greatest of our kin.

19.   However fate will pass, I surely see
that Brynhild's wrath surpasses reason's bounds!"

20.   "Let Guthorm be the one to end his life,
our younger brother, lacking sense or smarts!
He owes no oaths to Sigurð, nor his love,
we never swore we'd not incite another!"

21.   The reckless fool was glad to do the deed,
and so his blade went deep in Sigurð's heart.

22.   But Sigurð feared to flee, and sought revenge,
and flung a weapon at his foolish foe.
The gleaming blade of Gram went sailing forth
from Sigurð's hand to Guthorm's open back.

23.   His body split, and fell apart in halves;
his head and hands fell forward, with the blade,
his legs and feet fell backwards on the spot.

24.   While Guðrun soundly slept, at peace, in bed
at Sigurð's side, without a hint of hurt.
She woke to find her joys were swept away
by scarlet streams that gushed from princes' friend.

25.   She struck her heavy hands with such a boom
that Sigurð, strong of heart, arose in bed.
"Don't let your tears escape, my second soul,
so grievously, for still your brothers live!

26.   Our son is still too young to use his wits,
and does not know to hide from family!
I fear they're planning woe and death for him
and they have nearly settled on their schemes.

27.   You may have seven sons, but none will ride
as kin of yours when going to the Thing!
I think I know the source of all of this:
these twisted plots were born of Brynhild's mind!

28.   She loves me more than any other man,
but Gunnar has no grievances with me!
I kept our oaths, and loved him as my kin,
it can't be said that she's a "friend" of mine!"

29.   Then Guðrun sighed as Sigurð's life escaped,
she clasped her hands with such a roaring crack
that all the goblets rumbled on the shelves
and all the geese honked back from in the yard.

30.   Then Brynhild, Buðli's daughter, loudly laughed
a single time with all her frigid heart
when in her hall at last she heard the screams
and weeping wails of Gjuki's daughter's grief.

31.   Then Gunnar, lord of warriors, declared:
"You hateful witch, you do not laugh
because you're happy, or you know of good!
Your beauty fades, your face now fits the hurt
you've caused; I think your doom arrives!

32.   The only way you'd be a worthy girl
is if we cut down Atli in your sight!
If you should see your brother bleeding out
and try and fail to mend his mortal wounds!"

33.   "My Gunnar, you have shown your bravery,
but Atli does not fear your petty rage!
He'll draw his breaths a longer time than you,
your strength will never grow to match his own.

34.   I'll tell you now, although I know you know,
of how you brought this strife upon yourself!
I was not old, nor was I swelled with pride,
I had my share of wealth in Atli's hall.

35.   I had no urge for men to rule my life
before three kings on horseback sought my hand!
The sons of Gjuki and of Sigmund came
but should have stayed at home, and never come!

36.   Then Atli told me I would never have
the share of Hunnish wealth I'd rightly earned,
not land or gold, unless I married you!
I would not get the gold our fathers had,
the land that I was promised as a girl,
nor all the treasures that were rightly mine.

37.   My mind was roused, and muddled then with doubt
if I should fight and slaughter all of you
for Atli's sake, with courage in my coat.
Such bravery would soon be widely known
and break the wills of many valiant men.

38.   And so, we struck a deal, as nobles should,
I longed for more than men, but for the gold
and famous treasures Sigmund's son had gained,
no other's wealth would ever win my heart.

39.   From then, I swore that I would have the man
who rode on Grani's back, bedecked with gold!
His eyes were shining, not at all like yours,
you are like him in not a single way,
and yet you think you're equal men to him!

40.   Since then I've loved him only, no one else,
my heart is hardly like a whirling wheel!
But soon all this will reach my brother's ears
when he finds out I've led myself to death!

41.   I'm not so loose, or quite so weak of will
to have another's husband while I live.
He'll soon complete the vengeance I have sworn!"

42.   Then Gunnar, lord of armies, rose at last
and wrapped his arms around his lady's neck.
And those of every station came to her
with loving hearts, to talk her from the edge.

43.   But each of them were thrown from off her neck,
her heart was set to make the final trip.

44.   The brothers met alone, and Gunnar said:
"Our men must go together to the hall,
for there has never been a greater need!
We have to lead my wife away from death
before a greater evil comes for us!
Let's share our minds, and see what wisdom says."

45.   In answer Hogni said a single thing:
"I say we let her take the endless road,
and may she never see another birth!
She left her mother in a twisted shape,
that girl was born to trade in misery
and craft great pain and sorrow for mankind!"

46.   Then Gunnar left, his thoughts a dreary storm,
and found his wife distributing his gold.

47.   She glanced around at all the things she owned
and at the corpses of her slaughtered slaves,
with evil heart she donned her golden coat
and pierced her belly with a pointed blade.

48.   Her body slumped upon the pillow's edge,
with bloody heart she pondered all her schemes.

49.   "Now come," she said, "if you would claim
my gold or other lesser things from me!
I'll give you each a golden chain or gem
or clothes that shine or sheets as bright as day!"

50.   The hall fell silent as the women thought,
        and then in unison their voices called:
        "Enough have died, we have a life to live!
        We still have deeds of honor left to do!"

51.   And then the lady bound in linen sheets
        and few in years said wisely in response:
        "I do not want that those who'd rather live
        should lose their lives for me and me alone!

52.   But know that when your corpses go to burn
        there'll be no goods of Menja[107] there with you
        when you begin the trip to visit me!

53.   My Gunnar, sit, and I will tell you truth!
        Your lovely bride is soon to lose her life,
        your voyage soon will reach the open sea
        although my lungs will soon run out of breath!

54.   You'll mend things with your sister very soon,
        for you and her will find you truly share
        an equal sorrow over Sigurð's loss.

55.   She'll birth a girl, and raise her all alone,
        and call her Svanhild, she'll be widely known
        for beauty far beyond the golden sun.

56.   You'll give your sister to a noble man,
        that act will pierce the hearts of many men!
        She will not marry willingly, nor will
        she be a joyous wife in Atli's court,
        but nonetheless she'll be my brother's wife.

57.   For I remember much of how you all
        employed your treachery to win my hand,
        my will was hardly free when I drew breath!

---

[107] Gold.

58.   I see you'll lust for Oddrun as your wife,
        but Atli will not let you near the girl.
        In secret you will hold her in your arms,
        she'll love you as perhaps I should have done
        if we had been allowed a happy fate!

59.   I see that Atli's hate will end your life,
        he'll lay you out within a pit of snakes!

60.   And now I see that shortly after that
        my brother too will draw his final breath.
        He'll lose his joy and all the sons he loves,
        for Guðrun's blade will pierce him in his sleep
        as recompense against her wounded soul.

61.   It would be better if our sister would
        go with her husband to the halls of death,
        but none will counsel her so well as that
        and she is not as firm of heart as me!

62.   Now slowly I must speak, but next I see
        that though I wish it so, she will not die.
        The mighty waves will drag her far away
        to distant lands where Jonak's family rules.

63.   And Jonak's sons will take them in their care,
        and Svanhild will be sent to Gothic lands,
        the only living spawn of Sigurð's blood.

64.   But Bikki's words will be the death of her,
        for Jormunrekk has got a twisted heart.
        When all of Sigurð's kin have passed away,
        then Guðrun's grief will swell immensely more.

65.   There's one more thing I need to ask of you,
        my last request before I leave this world:
        I need a pyre, strong as any fort,
        out in the field, that's wide enough for all
        of us who've lost our lives for Sigurð's sake!

66.   May it be hung with shields and tapestries,
        with cloths of every shade and foreign slaves,
        may I be burnt with Sigurð at my side.

67.   And place that rippling blade between us both,
        that sharpened steel, the way it was before,
        the day we shared a bed, and when we seemed
        to be a happy, newly-married pair.

68.   The mighty door and all its gilded rings
        won't dare to strike the passing hero's heel,
        my followers will travel there with us,
        our journey there will be a blessed one!

69.   For thirteen servants travel out with us,
        and each of them is of a noble line.
        They grew with me, and were the greatest gift
        that Buðli gifted to his greatest girl.

70.   I've said a lot, and I would tell you more
        if fate had granted me more time to speak.
        My voice now fades, my wounds are swelling fast,
        I've told the truth, but now my life is gone!"

Helreið Brynhildar

Brynhild's Trip to Hell

Introduction

Helreið Brynhildar "Brynhild's Hell-Journey" is recorded in both the *Codex Regius* and the 14th-century *Norna-Gests Þáttr* "Norna-Gest's Story." It is the final poem to feature Brynhild.

The poem tells of an encounter between Brynhild and a devil woman during her journey to hell, which for the Norse was not necessarily a realm of punishment but simply the domain of the dead who were not chosen by Oðin or Freyja. Brynhild defends her actions in life, mirroring her speech in *Brynhildarkviða*, and her story concludes almost triumphantly, with her traveling to hell confident she will spend eternity with her love, Sigurð.

Helreið Brynhildar is likely among the youngest Eddic poems. This can be most clearly seen in the fact it places Sigurð in hell, when surely a warrior of his stature would be a shoo-in for Valhalla. This suggests the work of a Christian writer unfamiliar with how his pagan ancestors viewed the afterlife. Thus, the poem is most likely a product of the 12th century.

After Brynhild's death, two pyres were built. The first to burn was
Sigurð's, and the second, which had a wagon laden with expensive cloth,
was Brynhild's. Brynhild rode in this wagon on the road to hell, and
passed through the lands where a certain fiend woman lived. The fiend
said:

1. "You will not travel through my lands
enhanced with stone supports![108]
It's better if you weave a tapestry
than see another's man!

2. Why must you come from Valland here,
you fickle-minded girl?
You surely know you've washed the blood
of heroes from your hands!"

3. "Don't chastise me, you stony bride,
I'm on no Viking trip!
I'll seem the better of us both
to those who know our past!"

4. "You're Buðli's daughter, you were born
to suffer worst of all!
You've ruined all of Gjuki's kin
and knocked their houses down!"

5. "Then from my wagon I'll describe
to you, you witless girl,
how Gjuki's heirs destroyed my love
and made me break my oaths!

6. Beneath an oak eight sisters lost
their swan-cloaks to a king.
I was a girl, just twelve years old,
when he received my oaths.

7. I was well-known in Hlymdalir
as "Hild beneath the helm".

---

[108] Cliffs or mountains. Devils were believed to live inside stones.

300

8.   In Gothic lands I sent the old
king Hjalm-Gunnar to hell.
Thus Auða's brother won the fight
and earned me Oðin's wrath.

9.   He bound me up in Skatalund
with shields of red and white,
and said that I'd be woken up
by one who feels no fear.

10.   Around my hall in southern lands
he lit the bane of wood.[109]
No man but one could go across:
the one with Fafnir's gold.

11.   He rode on Grani with the gold
where Father ruled the seats.
The Danish Viking seemed the best
of all his retinue.

12.   We gladly slept beneath the sheets
as if he was my kin,
he did not place his hands on me
for eight long days and nights.

13.   Then Guðrun, Gjuki's daughter said
that Sigurð held me close,
and thus I learned what I should not:
my marriage was a lie!

14.   Our lives are short, but last too long,
and give us only pain!
I'll be with Sigurð evermore,
now sink, you devil-spawn!"

Then the fiend let out a terrible scream, and sank into the stone.

---

[109] Fire.

Dráp Niflunga

The Fall of the Niflungs

Introduction

Dráp Niflunga "The Niflungs' Deaths" is a short prose passage in the *Codex Regius* which serves as a narrative link between the series of poems about Sigurð and Brynhild and those about Atli's murder of Gunnar and Hogni.

Much like *Grípisspá*, it is almost certainly no older than the books in which these poems were first written, and is certainly a 13th-century creation.

Gunnar and Hogni claimed Fafnir's inheritance as their own.

After that, there was conflict between Atli and Gjuki's sons, as Atli blamed them for Brynhild's death. They agreed to settle the dispute by giving Guðrun to Atli in marriage, but she objected, and had to be fed a forgetting-potion before she would marry Atli. They had two sons together, named Erp and Eitill, and Atli also adopted Svanhild, Guðrun's daughter by Sigurð.

Gunnar wanted to marry Oddrun, Atli's sister, but Atli would not allow it. So he married Glaumvor instead, and Hogni married Kostbera. Between them, they had three sons: Solar, Saevar, and Gjuki.

Atli invited Gunnar and Hogni to his home, and sent a man named either Vingi or Knefroð[110] as his messenger. Knowing Atli's tricks, Guðrun sent runes warning them to stay away, and sent Hogni the ring Andvaranaut with wolf's hair tied around it.

When her brothers turned up anyway, Guðrun begged her sons to ask Atli to spare their uncles, but they refused. Hogni's heart was cut out, and Gunnar was thrown into a snake-pit. He played his harp and put the snakes to sleep, but one bit his liver and killed him.

---

[110] The man's name is Vingi in *Atlamál*, but Knefroð in *Atlakviða*.

306

Guðrúnarkviða II

Guðrun's Reflections

Introduction

This poem is also titled *Guðrúnarkviða* in the *Codex Regius*, though modern writers have titled it *Guðrúnarkviða II* to distinguish it from the earlier poem with that title.

Guðrúnarkviða II features Guðrun once again lamenting the troubles she has faced in life; both Sigurð's murder and her drug-induced marriage to Atli. The poem then jumps, for disputed reasons, to a series of grim nightmares Atli has been having, and of Guðrun's reassuring interpretations of them.

Many elements of this poem are closer to the recorded German stories than to the later Norse ones. Notably, Sigurð is said to be killed in the forest rather than his bed, and the motive for his murder is stated to be jealousy over social status. Brynhild, the instigator of Sigurð's murder in the other Norse poems, is barely mentioned, with her brothers being fully blamed for Sigurð's death. These similarities suggest the poem was composed closer in time to when the German tales reached Scandinavia, before the Norse adaptations were made. When this occurred is hard to say; *Fáfniskviða* may be a 10th-century poem, and Sigurð begins to appear on runestones around the 11th, so *Guðrúnarkviða II* may date from around that time.

King Þjoðrek came to visit Atli, having lost most of his men. He and
Guðrun mourned their losses together. She told him:

1.   "My mother raised the girl of girls
who loved her brothers much
till Gjuki showered me with gold
and made me Sigurð's wife.

2.   My Sigurð grew beyond my kin,
a leek above the grass,
a mighty stag above the beasts,
and gold among the silver.

3.   Until my brothers grew to loathe
the noble man I'd won.
They could not sleep or solve disputes
till Sigurð laid a corpse.

4.   With booming feet did Grani flee,
but Sigurð stayed behind.
The saddle-beast was soaked with sweat,
and he could labor hard.

5.   With soaking cheeks, I went to him
and asked the horse for news.
But Grani merely bowed his head,
he knew his lord was dead.

6.   My mind was split, I thought a while,
then asked about my love.

7.   But Gunnar only drooped his head,
then Hogni told the truth:
"We cut our brother's killer down,
he's now a wolf's dessert!

8.   You'll find him on the southern road,
where happy ravens scream
and eagles too, at sight of food,
and howling wolves around him!"

9.   "Why would you boast of such a deed
        and steal my joy away?
        May ravens rip your heart apart
        across the boundless earth!"

10.   Then Hogni said a single thing,
        his heart still flush with grief:
        "My sister, you will grieve the more
        if ravens shred my heart!"

11.   I turned alone from his reply
        and got the scraps of wolves.
        I did not wail or clasp my hands
        or mourn as women do,
        I sat there, dead as Sigurð was.

12.   The moon was always new at night
        when by my man I sat.
        I would have loved the wolves the most
        if they would take my life
        or burn me up like birch!

13.   And then I turned, five days I fled,
        till Half's high hall I reached.

14.   Three years, plus half, I stayed in Denmark
        with Þora, Hakon's girl.
        To keep me sane, she wove with gold
        Dane swans and southern halls.

15.   We sewed in cloth the games of men
        and princes and their thanes
        and crimson shields and swords and helms
        of Hunnish retinues,

16.   the ships of Sigmund leaving shore
        with gleaming figureheads,
        and on the edge, he fought his foes
        in Fif, across the sea.

17.   Then Grimhild heard in Gothic halls
that I was still depressed.
She cast her weaving to the side
and asked her sons with force
to compensate their sister for
my son and fallen man.

18.   And Gunnar gladly offered gold
and Hogni did as well.
She asked them then to mount their steeds
and leash them to a cart,
to ride their horses, fly a hawk,
and fire bows of yew.

19.   Then Valdar, king of Danes, arrived
with Jaroslav in tow,
and Eymoð came with Jarizskar
and crimson Lombard cloaks,
with armor, blades, and mighty helms,
and hair of darkest brown.

20.   They all had come with gifts for me
and many honeyed words,
they sought to soothe my many pains
but could not gain my trust.

21.   So Grimhild fetched for me a horn,
its liquid bitter cold,
and mingled with the might of fate
and sea and blood of boars.

22.   Inside the horn were scarlet runes
which I could hardly read,
a serpent of the Hadding lands
and grain and guts of beasts.

23.   That beer was bound with evil things
and ash from roots and acorns,
and dew that falls from burning hearths[111]
for it resolves disputes.

---

[111] Soot.

24.   It made us all forget our hates
        when we consumed it there.
        Three kings then knelt before my knees,
        and Grimhild said to me:

25.   "My daughter, I have gold for you
        which Gjuki used to own,
        the finest hoard from Hloðver's halls
        for Sigurð's poor demise.

26.   The Hunnish girls who weave the best
        of cloth will bring you joy!
        You'll have the wealth of Buðli's kin,
        for you'll be Atli's wife!"

27.   "I'll never marry Brynhild's kin
        or any other man!
        It would be wrong to birth his heirs
        or love my life with him!"

28.   "Don't take your sorrows out on men,
        the fault is ours alone!
        It will be like the Volsungs live
        when you give birth to sons."

29.   "I cannot rush to claim a man
        and think he'll give me joy
        When Oðin's ravens made a feast
        of Sigurð's bloody heart!"

30.   "But Atli is a noble man,
        the best in all the lands!
        You'll have him till your hair is grey
        or you will die alone!"

31.   "Do not insist on sending me
        to such a hateful union!
        I've seen that he'll do Gunnar harm
        and cut out Hogni's heart!
        I will not rest until I take
        that butcher's life away!"

32.   Then Grimhild wept at what I said,
for she knew it was true.
She'd seen an evil fate ahead
for both the sons she'd raised.

33.   "I'll give you lands and all their men,
if you'll accept them now.
So hold them close and love them well
and cherish them, my girl!"

34.   "Then I will have him, it's the wish
of everyone but me!
He will not bring me any joy,
nor will my kin be safe!"

35.   Then men were lifted on their steeds,
and women on the carts.
A week we rode through freezing land,
another on the waves,
a third through arid fields.

36.   The keepers of the looming walls
allowed us in the court.

37.   I still was flush with hateful thoughts
about my brothers' deaths
when Atli woke me up.

38.   "The Norns have roused me from my sleep
with dreams of misery!
I dreamed your heart was treacherous,
your blade was stuck in mine!"

39.   "A dream of iron leads to flame,
a woman's wrath to pride.
I'll always cauterize your wounds
although I hate your guts!"

40.   "I dreamed of shoots all shriveled brown,
that I had hope to grow.
Their roots were torn, stained red with blood,
and yet I ate them whole!

41.   I dreamed of hawks in evil lands
        in search of tasty meat.
        I ate their hearts with honeyed blood
        and very gloomy thoughts!

42.   I dreamed of puppies running loose
        and howling, free of joy.
        I had to eat their rotten flesh
        against my own free will!"

43.   "You dreamed of future sacrifice,
        of little heads removed.
        They're doomed to die in coming days,
        and be a meal for lords!"

44.   Then in the deathbed I laid down
        without the need for sleep,
        this I remember well.

Guðrúnarkviða III

Guðrun's Ordeal

Introduction

The shortest poem of the entire Edda, *Guðrúnarkviða III* tells a brief tale of Guðrun's trial by ordeal after a false accusation of adultery by one of her husband's former lovers. Trial by ordeal was a common way in the Middle Ages to test the guilt of an accused criminal. The accused was tasked with pulling some object, usually a stone, from boiling water, obviously scalding the hands. The accused's hands would then be bandaged for three days, and if they were visibly healing after that time, the accused was innocent; if not, they were guilty.

This subject makes the poem fairly easy to date; trial by ordeal is known to have reached Scandinavia in the early 11th century. Atli calling for a Saxon priest to consecrate the water suggests the practice was still seen as foreign to the poem's intended audience. It seems this poem was made to introduce a foreign judicial practice using existing mythology, and thus it certainly is from the early 11th century.

Herkja was one of Atli's maids, and had once been his lover. She told him she had seen Þjoðrek and Guðrun together. Atli was furious about this. Guðrun said to him:

1.   "What's wrong, my Atli, Buðli's son,
your mind is dark, you never laugh!
You ought to speak with other men
but always keep your gaze on me!

2.   "It hurts me, Guðrun, Gjuki's girl,
that Herkja told me in the hall
you shared a bed with Þjoðrek once
and laid with him in linen sheets!"

3.   "I'll swear an oath of honesty
upon the sacred, pearly stone,
I did no thing with Þjoðmar's son
that men and women tend to do!

4.   I spoke with him a single time
without another man around.
We did not think of melding flesh,
instead we shared our deepest pains.

5.   Recall, he came with thirty men,
and not a single one still breathes!
They're like my brothers in their mail,
they shared the fate of all my kin!"

6.   "Let's send for Saxi from the south!
He'll consecrate the boiling pot!"

7.   Eight-forty men were watching there
when Guðrun reached into the pot.

8.   "I cannot ask my brothers' aid,
I know I won't see them again!
For Hogni would defend my name,
but now I must defend myself!"

9.   Her hands then dove into the pot
        and lifted out the shining stones.
        "Now all may see I'm innocent,
        the holy cauldron boils hot!"

10.   Then Atli laughed with joyous heart
        when Guðrun's hands emerged untouched.
        "Now let's have Herkja try the pot,
        the one who's lied about my wife!"

11.   There never was a fouler sight
        than Herkja's steaming, scalded hands!
        They drowned her in a stinking bog
        as recompense for Guðrun's harms.

Oddrúnargrátr

Oddrun's Lament

Introduction

Oddrúnargrátr "Oddrun's Lament" appears with no title in the *Codex Regius*; its modern title comes from its final stanza instead.

This poem briefly interrupts the Niflung series to briefly tell the story of Oddrun, Atli and Brynhild's sister and Gunnar's lover, and her rescue of the heavily pregnant princess Borgny. It is implied that these two have history, but any other stories about either of them have been lost; Oddrun is briefly referenced in *Dráp Niflunga* and *Brynhildarkviða*, and Borgny is mentioned nowhere else.

There is no equivalent to Oddrun in any of the surviving German stories, which raises the possibility that she is a Norse addition. If so, the poem is likely a later work, perhaps from the 11th century.

There once was a woman named Borgny, daughter of king Heiðrek. She was impregnated by her lover, Vilmund, but could not give birth until Oddrun, Atli's sister, who had been Gunnar's lover, came to see her. This story was written about the visit.

1.   I heard it told in ancient tales
of girls in Mornaland
how none who dwell upon the earth
could ease poor Borgny's pain.

2.   Then Oddrun, Atli's sister, heard
about the woman's pain.
She fetched a horse from Hunnish stalls
and saddled up its back.

3.   She rode across the earthen road
until she reached a hall
both long and high, and went inside.
She yanked the saddle off the steed
and then she said these words aloud:

4.   "What is the news in Hunnish lands
that's worth discussing here?"
"Your friend is here in birthing-pain,
do you know how to help?"

5.   "What man has made her suffer so?
Who's made poor Borgny writhe?"

6.   "His name is Vilmund, friend of hawks,
five years he laid her down in sheets,
her father had no clue."

7.   Those two then shared no further words,
then Oddrun knelt beside her.
She chanted spells with might and strength,
for Borgny, bitter spells.

8.   A boy and girl then walked the earth
the kin of Hogni's bane.
Though she'd been quiet very long,
the weakened woman said:

9.   "May friendly spirits keep you safe,
          and Frigg and Freyja too,
          since you have made my sorrows end!"

10.   "I did not come and give you aid
          because you've earned it, girl!
          I made a promise in this place
          that I would render aid
          as long as noble lines endure."

11.   "You've lost it, Oddrun, gone insane,
          to speak to me like that!
          Though I went with you through the world,
          as if our blood was shared!"

12.   "Remember what you said to me
          when I made Gunnar drinks?
          You said no girl did such a thing
          except for me alone."[112]

13.   Then Oddrun sat, her heart in shards,
          and spoke of all her pains:

14.   I grew up in a happy hall
          where I was well adored.
          I made the most of Father's gifts
          five winters, while he lived.

15.   My weary father ordered this,
          before his breath ran out:
          that I should get a golden hoard
          and marry Grimhild's son.

16.   And Brynhild ought to wear a helm
          and be a valkyrie.
          If she was spared by fate, he said,
          there'd be no nobler girl.

---

[112] Apparently, Borgny figured out Oddrun and Gunnar's affair, and scolded her for it. A deeply ironic turn of events, considering her current situation.

17.   But Brynhild wove her tapestries
        of lands and noble men.
        The earth and sky were both alight
        when Fafnir's bane arrived.

18.   They fought a war with foreign blades,
        and shattered Brynhild's walls.
        And shortly after all had passed,
        she learned the Gjukungs' tricks.

19.   Her vengeance then was cruel and swift,
        of that enough's been said!
        But soon all men will hear of how
        in Sigurð's name she died!

20.   Then I gave Gunnar all my love
        as Brynhild should have done.

21.   They offered Atli quite a hoard
        of wealth beyond compare
        from Grani's back, and fifteen farms
        if I'd be Gunnar's wife.

22.   But Atli said he'd never give
        his kin to Gjuki's boys.
        But I held Gunnar in my arms,
        we could not hide our needs.

23.   My kin then started gossiping
        and said I'd been with him,
        but Atli said I'd do no deed
        to shame our family.

24.   But anyone would shame their kin
        when love becomes involved!

25.   So Atli's scouts then followed me
        to test my loyalty.
        They found us where they shouldn't have,
        beneath a linen sheet.

26.   We offered them a hefty bribe
        to keep the truth from him,
        but they went home in quite a rush
        and told him everything.

27.   'Twas only Guðrun was not told,
        the one who should have known.

28.   Their gilded horse thundered loud
        when Gjuki's boys arrived.
        Then Hogni's heart was taken out
        and Gunnar laid with snakes.

29.   Of course, this happened while I was
        at Geirmund's making feasts!
        But Gunnar sadly played his harp,
        he thought I'd come to help.

30.   I heard in Hlesey how his strings
        were screaming in distress,
        I told my maids to get me home
        so I could save his life!

31.   Our ship then sailed across the sound
        till we reached Atli's lands.

32.   But Atli's mother[113] slithered in,
        and may that woman rot!
        She dug her fangs in Gunnar's heart,
        and thus my love was doomed!

33.   I've often wondered why it is
        that still I cling to life
        without brave Gunnar, lord of blades,
        who I loved like myself!

---

[113] The snake that killed Gunnar. This might be either Atli's mother magically morphed
into a snake, or Oddrun insulting her own mother.

34.   You've sat and listened as I spoke
        of all my grief, and theirs.
        Desire drives us all to live!
        Now my lament is done!"

Atlakviða

The Death of Atli

Introduction

Atlakviða "Atli's Poem", probably wrongly titled *Atlakviða in Grǿnlenzka* "Atli's Poem in Greenlandic" in the *Codex Regius*, continues the Niflung story after the previous two poems' interruption. It tells the story of Atli's murder of Gunnar and Hogni, and Guðrun's bloody vengeance against him.

Despite its *Regius* name, the poem likely predates the 985 Norse settlement of Greenland, and is likely among the oldest poems in the Edda. The Greenlandic attribution was probably a result of confusion with *Atlamál*, the next poem in the *Regius*.

There are several clues pointing to *Atlakviða*'s advanced age. The first is that, like some other Eddic poems, it contains cases of *reið* allterating with *v*-initial words, which indicates it must predate the 11th century.

Another hint is its meter; its lines have much looser syllabic restrictions, which as mentioned in *Hlǫðskviða*'s introduction is a sign of an older poem.

The final sign of the poem's age is that Sigurð goes totally unmentioned. This is significant when one considers the historical events that seem to have inspired these poems; Gunnar's death is likely based on the eradication of the Burgundian kingdom under King Gundahar by a Roman-Hunnish army under Flavius Aetius in the 5th century, while the Frankish kings that likely inspired Sigurð lived in the 6th. This means that the former story was told for at least a century without the involvement of Sigurð, and his sudden disappearance from a series of poems where he had previously been so significant suggests that this poem may preserve a much older tradition. All this evidence points to a date in the 8th or 9th century.

It has become well-known how Guðrun, daughter of Gjuki, avenged the murder of her brothers. She killed Atli's sons, then Atli himself, and burned down his hall. This poem was written about these events.

1. In early days, a man named Knefroð rode
from Atli's hall with news for Gjuki's boys.
He met with Gunnar there in Gjuki's hall,
around the hearth they drank his sweetened beer.

2. His soldiers joined them, kept their fear concealed,
and sipped their wine within the slaughter-hall,
then Knefroð called, his voice as cold as ice,
reverberating from the highest bench:

3. "My lord has sent me on my hustling horse
across the famous forest known as Murkwood,
to ask that Gjuki's sons come visit him
and hang their helms in Atli's mighty hall!

4. He'll give you shields and shaven spears of ash,
and golden helms and Hunnish warriors,
and silver saddles, shirts as red as blood,
and lances, spears, and hustling horses too.

5. He said he'd give you all of Gnitaheið,
and screaming spears and gilded stems of boats,
and prosperous steads along the Dneiper's banks,
and all the famous trees of Murkwood too!"

6. King Gunnar looked to Hogni then, and said:
"What shall we make of such an offering?
There are no treasures on Gnitaheið
the likes of which we don't already have!

7. We each have seven houses, stuffed with swords,
the hilt of each is lined with purest gold.
I have the fastest horse, the sharpest sword,
the strongest bows, and armor lined with gold.
My helm and shield have come from Roman halls,
there's nothing like them in the Hunnish lands!"

8.   "I got a ring from Guðrun yesterday,"
said Hogni, "with wolf hair on the band.
I think she sent a warning with the ring,
we'll walk the path of wolves, if we should go!"

9.   No man urged Gunnar go, nor kin of his,
no counselor would dare advise this course,
but Gunnar spoke the way a ruler should,
with glory and with passion in his hall:

10.   "Arise now, Fjornir, let the golden cups
sit in the hands of every person here!

11.   May wolves control the Gjukungs' golden hoard
until they grey, if I do not return!
The Niflung bears will bite with mangling teeth
and give the Hunnish bitches quite a fight!

12.   Then Gunnar's weeping retinue arrived,
they left their cubs behind and traveled far,
and Hogni's youngest said a final thing:
"May wit and wisdom guide you where you go!"

13.   The Niflungs led their steeds across the peaks
and galloped hard through Murkwood's gloomy shade.
All Hunland thundered where their forces passed,
where stick-shy horses crossed the verdant plains.

14.   They saw the hall, its moats and battlements,
and Buðli's soldiers standing all around.
They saw the southern hall, its ring of seats,
its shining wall of shield-rims, side by side.

15.   Amid the spears and standards Atli sat
and sipped his wine within the slaughter-hall.
Like hawks his guards watched Gunnar's every move,
in case he wakened war with screaming spears.

16.   Their sister saw them come into the hall
and called to them, her mind not fogged with beer:
"You've been betrayed, there's nothing you can do
to leave alive, unless you flee at once!

17.   You should have come here in a coat of mail
         and sturdy helm, to visit Atli's hall!
         You should have spent today atop your horse
         and grieved the Norns with hills of pallid dead,
         and sent the Hunnish ladies home in chains,
         and hurled my husband in his pit of snakes,
         instead it's you who'll die in serpents' halls!"

18.   "It's far too late to call the Niflungs here,
         our bravest men are but a distant sight,
         the ruddy hills of home are far away!"

19.   The friends of Burgundy seized Gunnar fast
         and bound him tightly with the firmest chains.

20.   But Hogni's savage sword slew seven men,
         he plunged an eighth in Atli's searing hearth,
         he gave his all to keep his brother safe
         the way all noble men should shield their kin.

21.   They came to Gunnar first, the valiant king,
         to see if he would trade his hoard to live.

22.   "You'll get it if you give me Hogni's heart,
         cut out from him with brutal, biting blade,
         stained red with dripping royal blood!"

23.   But first they cut the heart from Hjalli's chest,
         and Gunnar got it on a silver plate.

24.   Then Gunnar, lord of men, declared to them:
         "You fools, I see that this is Hjalli's heart
         and not my noble brother Hogni's heart!
         Like leaves in wind it trembles on the plate,
         it shuddered twice as much inside his chest!"

25.   The smith of wounds let out a hearty laugh
         when Hunnish thugs arrived to carve him up!
         He did not think to cry, or beg for life,
         and Gunnar got it on a silver plate.

26.   Then Gunnar, valiant Nifling lord, declared:
"I see this is the valiant Hogni's heart,
and not a coward's heart, like Hjalli was!
It only shakes a bit upon the plate
and trembled even less inside his chest!

27.   Now Atli soon will be as far from sight
as he will be from any gold of mine,
for I alone can find the Niflungs' gold
with Hogni now a bloody, heartless corpse!

28.   I feared you'd learn the truth while Hogni lived,
since I alone still breathe, I fear no more!
The Rhine will have my hoard forevermore,
its currents will control the holy hoard,
the Niflungs' gold will glow in surging streams,
and not upon the arms of Hunnish dogs!"

29.   "Bring out the wagons! Lead this man to death!"

30.   Then Atli mounted up his noisy steed
with thorns of battle on his every side,
while Guðrun prayed to gods of victory
and battled tears within the chaos-hall.

31.   "May Atli be betrayed as he betrayed
the oaths he swore to Gunnar long ago
upon the southern sun and Sigtyr's rock,
on resting-horses and the ring of Ull!"

32.   Then horses dragged the guard of gold away,
and brought the lord of battle to his death.

33.   A Hunnish host then laid him in a pit,
the serpents' home, whose floor was never still,
whose bottom was concealed by coiled snakes.
But Gunnar struck his harp, his hateful thoughts
resounding in the echo of the strings,
and thus must noble men defend what's theirs!

34.   Then Atli turned and led his men away
across the land, and left the murder scene.
Their steeds were packed so tight as they returned,
their weapon-song rang out through Atli's court.

35.   Then Guðrun met her husband at the gate
to compensate him with a golden cup:
"Accept from me, my husband, in your hall,
a feast of young ones, gone to misty halls!"[114]

36.   Then Atli's goblets, laden much with wine,
resounded as the bearded warriors
were gathered in his hall to celebrate.

37.   And Guðrun, beautiful and terrible,
prepared the tables, made them beer and snacks.
She had no choice but feed her pale-faced foes,
and then to Atli said these evil words:

38.   "Enjoy your meal, my lord? You have consumed
the hearts of both your sons, with honey glaze!
Your Majesty's digesting childrens' meat,
you served them to your guests as snacks with beer!

39.   You won't call Erp or Eitill to your lap
or hear the joyous laughter of your sons!
You'll never see them in your hall again,
you'll never see your princes shaping spears
or trimming manes, or spurring on their steeds!"

40.   A din erupted, and a mourning-song,
the Huns were wailing in their fancy cloth,
while only Guðrun had no sodden eyes,
not for her brothers or her little boys,
the ones she birthed and put on Atli's plate!

---

[114] Guðrun alludes to animal sacrifice. Young animals tended to be the ones picked for this. In truth, of course, she refers to Atli's sons.

41.   Then Guðrun, bright as goslings, scattered gold
        and gifted rings to all of Atli's slaves.
        She sprouted seeds of fate, let metal flow,
        and did not spare the temples of the gods!

42.   And Atli, deadly drunk, was unaware,
        he had no blade and did not fear his wife.
        He much preferred to hold his lady close
        and show her off to all his noblemen!

43.   Then Guðrun's dagger fed the mattress blood,
        she stained it red with hands that longed for hell!
        She freed his dogs and warned his slaves to flee,
        then cast a burning brand into the hall,
        and thus earned justice for her brothers' deaths!

44.   She fed the flames with everyone inside
        who'd come from Murkheim and from Gunnar's death.
        The ancient timbers fell, and temples smoked,
        the Hunnish farms and all their shield-maids burned
        they sank and roasted in the searing flame.

45.   And thus the tale is told! No girl will go
        in armor to avenge her kin again!
        Three kings were ended by the woman's deeds
        before she joined them in the halls of hell.

The Greenlanders tell this story in more detail.

Atlamál in Grønlenzku

The Death of Atli, as told in Greenland

Introduction

"The Greenlanders tell this story in more detail", says the *Codex Regius*. On this, *Atlamál in Grønlenzku* "Atli's Words in Greenlandic" certainly delivers; its 104 stanzas make it the second-longest poem in the Edda, coming in behind only *Hávamál*. However, while that poem is clearly a compilation, *Atlamál* is a single, continuous narrative told at great length- an impressive accomplishment for an orally composed poem.

Atlamál tells a different variation of the story told in *Atlakviða*, sacrificing the drama and evocative imagery of that poem for more detailed examination of the personalities and motivations of its characters.

Unlike *Atlakviða*, there is reason to believe *Atlamál* may have actually been composed in Greenland; notably, it contains a vivid description of a polar bear, an animal a Norseman could only see in Greenland. Also, Atli's force of thirty retainers would have been laughably tiny even in Iceland, let alone on the continent, but would have been more reasonable in the sparsely populated Greenlandic settlements. If so, the poem cannot predate 986, the year the Norse colonization of Greenland began. However, Guðrun's description of death as "another light" suggests Christian influence, meaning the poem was likely composed after the Christianization of Greenland in the 11th century.

1.   All men have heard of ills that grew
        from secret Hunnish Things!
        It earned for them and Gjuki's sons
        no good, but fear and death.

2.   They guided princes to their doom,
        which should have never been!
        Though Atli should have used his wits,
        he brought about his end.

3.   But Guðrun, wise and sharp of wit,
        observed their secret plans.
        She sought to spare her brothers' lives
        before they crossed the sea.

4.   And so she carved them warning-runes,
        but Vingi twisted them.
        Then Atli's vicious messenger
        sailed over Limafjord.

5.   They welcomed him and lit the hearth,
        and thought he had no tricks.
        They took the gifts that Atli sent
        and hung them without thought.

6.   Then Hogni's woman, Kostbera,
        and Glaumvor, Gunnar's wife,
        stepped out with smiles in the hall
        and tended to their guest.

7.   He first asked Hogni if he'd go,
        his tricks were obvious!
        For Gunnar would if Hogni did,
        and Hogni said he'd go.

8.   They brought out mead, and feasted much,
        till they were stuffed with drink.
        Then all the couples went to bed,
        and soundly fell asleep.

9.   Except for Kostbera, who read the runes
        by flashing firelight.
        She had to keep her speech concealed,
        and they were hard to read.

10.   She then joined Hogni in his bed
        and dreamed a nasty dream.
        She sought the prince when he awoke
        and told him all she'd seen:

11.   "If you would go, then heed my words,
        and go another time!
        I read the runes your sister carved,
        she's warned you: stay away!

12.   There's still one thing I cannot tell:
        what made her carve them wrong?
        It seems to go will be your death,
        but there's a missing rune."

13.   "A woman's heart is full of fear,
        but mine is not," said Hogni,
        "I will not seek the things you've seen
        except to pay them back,
        for Atli's gold will soon be ours,
        I don't fear what I've heard!"

14.   "If you should go, then you will fall,
        you won't be greeted well!
        I will not hide the things I've dreamed,
        your oars will fight the stream.

15.   I saw your bed consumed with flame,
        it spread throughout the house!
        The linen cloths you care not for
        will soon be up in smoke.

16.   A bear came in and broke the beams,
        and waved its lumbering paws!
        It pinned us all inside its jaws,
        its steps made booming waves!"

17.   "The flame's a sign that wind will come
before the break of dawn.
A snow-white bear means storms will come,
a blizzard from the east."

18.   "I dreamed an eagle flew in here
and splattered us with blood!
It seemed like Atli's spirit-shape,[115]
I think he'll give us grief!"

19.   "We'll soon see blood from slaughtered beasts,
and eagles stand for cows.
Despite your dreams, the man's no threat!"
No further words were said.

20.   The same occurred when Gunnar woke
beside his well-born wife,
for Glaumvor feared her dreams' events,
and Gunnar brushed her off.

21.   "I saw you hanging from a noose
above a pit of snakes!
They ate your flesh, I lost my man,
the gods' demise arrived!"

[There is likely a missing stanza here in which Gunnar interprets this dream, but the *Volsunga Saga* lacks any counterpart to it].

22.   "I dreamed of blood upon your shirt,
that is a harmful sign!
I saw a spear wedged in your side,
and howling wolves each way!"

23.   "You dreamed of dogs, they bark a lot
before the flight of spears."

24.   "A river flowed across the hall,
its fury drowned the seats,
its currents broke your brothers' legs,
the water never stilled.

---

[115] People's spirits were believed to have animal shapes.

[There is likely a missing stanza here in which Gunnar interprets this dream. In the *Volsunga Saga*, Gunnar says this dream foretells a bountiful harvest.]

25.   The ghosts of ladies came tonight
and asked to visit you,
They sought that you would sit with them,
your disir[116] have no strength!"

26.   "It's far too late for argument,
my fate has long been fixed.
I can't escape it, I must go,
although I'll surely die!"

27.   They all arose by morning's light,
but should have been restrained!
Five men went on this foolish trip,
and twice that number stayed.
Snaevar and Solar went with them,
brave Hogni's little boys,
and kindly Orkning went with them,
the kin of Kostbera.

28.   Their women went with them a ways
until they reached a fjord.
They pleaded for their men to stay,
but none would hear them out.

29.   Then Glaumvor, Gunnar's wife, declared
to Vingi, eyes aflame:
"Recall that evil to a guest
will bring an evil fate!"

30.   "May fiends consume him if he's lied,"
swore Vingi's lying tongue.
"May Atli dangle from a rope
if he mistreats his guests!"

---

[116] Elsewhere in the *Edda*, this term refers to the Norns, but here it seems to describe female guardian spirits, possibly ancestral spirits, warning of Gunnar's impending death.

31.   And Bera told her man with love:
"Sail well, earn victory!
May none prevent your coming home,
may all go well for you!"

32.   And Hogni's answer came with love:
"Take solace in my fate,
no matter how it comes to pass!
I've often heard it said
that men don't care how they leave home,
but now I know it's false."

33.   They shared a gaze, then parted ways,
and fate then split their roads.

34.   They rowed so hard they smashed the keel,
the motion strained their backs,
the oar-holes burst, the rowlocks split,
they left the boat adrift.

35.   And then they came to Buðli's lands,
I'll tell this to the end!
When Hogni beat the sturdy gates,
they made a mighty clank.

36.   Then Vingi spoke, but shouldn't have:
"My kind request was born from lies,
keep out of Atli's house!
For soon you both will burn alive,
we'll quickly cut you down!
I'll make a gallows for you both,
if you should calmly wait!"

37.   But Hogni feared to flee, and said,
quite keen to test himself:
"We do not fear you, or your case!
Your words have brought you death!"

38.   Then Vingi joined the host of Hel,
his breaths were met with blows.

39.   Then Atli met them with his men,
        they stood a fence away.
        Then hateful words were flung about:
        "I've longed to end your lives!"

40.   "I have to say, it's hard to tell
        if you have planned this out!
        You're unprepared, and Vingi's dead,
        we've given him to Hel!"

41.   The Huns were frenzied at the prince's words
        and firmly gripped their bows.
        They hid behind a wall of shields
        and shot with all their might.

42.   The slaves then whispered in the house
        of outside's happenings.

43.   Then Guðrun frenzied at the news
        and cast her jewels aside.
        Her silver scattered on the floor
        and all her rings were smashed.

44.   She went outside, and split the doors
        so she could welcome guests.
        She greeted them a final time
        and told them many truths:

45.   "I tried to keep you far from here,
        but none can flee their fate!"
        She pleaded that a peace be made,
        but none would welcome that.

46.   She saw their battle would be harsh,
        so threw her cloak away.
        She joined her brothers in the fight,
        not kind was she in war.

47.   Two Huns were slain by Gjuki's girl,
        another lost his leg.
        She crippled Atli's brother there,
        and he was carried off.

48.   Another never rose again
        when Guðrun struck him down.
        She sent him to the hall of Hel
        with hands as firm as stone.

49.   The Niflungs fought a vicious fight
        that matched their noblest deeds!
        They shredded armor, shattered helms,
        their courage never failed.

50.   They battled through the afternoon
        until the break of dawn.
        By noon, the field was drenched with blood
        and eighteen Huns lay dead.
        Kostbera's brother fell there, too,
        and also both her sons.

51.   Then Atli said with burning rage:
        "This evil comes from you!
        I once had thirty noble thanes,
        but just eleven live!

52.   When Buðli died, he had five sons,
        but half have gone to hell,
        and two have lost their limbs!

53.   I cannot lie, your kin are strong,
        but you're an evil bride!
        I've had no quiet since you came.
        and gained no joy from you!
        You stole my gold and killed my kin,
        and caused my sister's death!"

54.   "That's rich indeed to hear from you,
        These evil deeds are yours!
        You starved my cousin in a cave
        and killed my mom for gold!
        Your suffering's a joke to me,
        for it, I thank the gods!"

55.   "My thanes, ensure my wife's in pain,
        I want to hear her scream!
        Do everything to make her cry,
        I'll see her miserable!

56.   Let's carve a hole in Hogni's chest,
        and cut his heart from him!
        We'll dangle Gunnar from a rope
        and call the snakes to him."

57.   Then Hogni said, "Do what you will!
        I've suffered worse than this!
        You cannot harm us when we're well,
        but only when we're hurt!"

58.   Then Beiti, Atli's steward, said:
        "Let Hjalli die instead!
        That lazy fool has lived too long,
        and fate's decreed his death!"

59.   The guard of pots then ran and hid,
        for weakness was his way.
        "The fault of war is theirs alone,
        why should I pay the price?
        I should be slaughtered with my pigs
        and praised for all my work!"

60.   They thrust a knife at Buðli's cook,
        the slave screamed at the sight.
        He said he'd gladly scatter shit
        on every inch of field,
        he'd do the nastiest of work
        if they would spare his life.

61.   Then Hogni pled for Hjalli's life,
        there's few so brave as that!
        "I'd rather this be done to me,
        who wants to hear him squeal?"

62.   They seized and bound the noble one,
for fate could not be stalled.
And all the world heard Hogni laugh,
he did not fear his end.

63.   While Gunnar dangled from a rope,
his toes could pluck his harp.
The men cried out who heard him sing,
his song made women weep.

64.   Although they died before midday,
their fame will never die.

65.   Then Atli, flush with victory,
began to taunt his wife:
"The morning's here, your kin are not,
the fault for it is yours!"

66.   "I'm sure you're happy to announce it,
but soon you will regret it!
I'll tell you what your fate will be:
as long as I draw breath,
great evil's all you'll know!"

67.   "I can't deny that, but I can
suggest a better course:
with slaves and gems, or what you wish,
I'll compensate your loss."

68.   "I've broken oaths for less than this,
I will not take your bribes!
I only tolerated you
while Hogni still drew breath!
If you thought I was harsh before,
the worst is yet to come!

69.   We sprouted in a single house
and played beneath its shade,
and Grimhild gave us rings and torcs
that cannot be replaced.
No gold atones for what I've lost
or makes me feel at ease!

70.   But women's freedom always falls
        before the might of men
        as kings must stoop and bow their heads
        when all their pawns have died,
        or trees will tumble to the earth
        when someone steals their roots!
        Thus, Atli, you may freely rule
        the things that happen here!"

71.   He shouldn't have believed her words,
        her treachery was plain!
        For Guðrun fought with both her shields[117]
        and set a twisted trap.

72.   She held a feast to hail her kin,
        and Atli for his men.

73.   They said no more, and readied beer,
        the men got rowdy drunk.
        Then Guðrun tortured Buðli's kin
        with vengeance past the pale.

74.   She lured her children to a bench,
        they had no fear or tears.
        They nestled in their mother's arms
        and asked what she had planned.

75.   "Don't be afraid, my little ones,
        for now you'll never age!"

76.   "There's none to stop you from this act,
        but know you'll gain no peace!"

77.   Their childhoods were then stopped short
        by cuts across their necks!
        When Atli couldn't find his boys,
        he asked where they had gone.

---

[117] An idiom equivalent to "spoke out of both sides of her mouth."

78.   "I won't conceal their fate from you,
       it will not bring you joy!
       You roused my wrath the day you slew
       my brothers in your hall!

79.   I've hardly slept since they've been gone,
       I promised agony!
       You taunted me at morning-time,
       and now, at night, you'll know!

80.   Your sons are gone, as you deserve,
       their skulls contained your beer!
       The drinks you drank all through the night
       were blended with their blood!

81.   I took their hearts and roasted them,
       and told you it was kid!
       You ate your children by yourself,
       and trusted in your teeth!

82.   There's none who'd ask for such a fate,
       I'd never boast of it,
       though I admit my part."

83.   "What sort of person are you, girl,
       to execute your sons
       and blend their blood into a drink?
       You've spared me little pain!"

84.   "If I could kill you, too, I would,
       it's more than you deserve!
       You've long surpassed the rest of men
       in foolishness and wrath
       and now exceeded even that,
       you've made your mourning feast!"

85.   "I'll have you stoned and burnt to death
       and thus you'll get your wish!"

86.   "I'll leave this life a better way,
       but say what helps you sleep!"

87.   They stayed together, steeped in hate,
and neither was content.
Then Hniflung's heart swelled up with wrath,
with her he hatched a plot.

88.   For Guðrun thought of Hogni's fate,
and felt revenge was just.
She quickly struck, with Hogni's son,
they didn't sit and wait.

89.   Their blows roused Atli from his sleep,
he sensed that he would die.
He said, "Who's murdered Buðli's son?
I sense great treachery!"

90.   "I won't conceal the truth from you
before your breath runs out.
Our names are Guðrun, Grimhild's girl,
and Hniflung, Hogni's son."

91.   "You've stooped to murdering your friends
who've placed their faith in you!
I only went to seek your hand
at others' urging, girl!

92.   A noble widow, I was told,
that surely was no lie!
I brought you here with much rejoicing,
we seemed so happy then.

93.   Our nobles were the best of men,
we thronged with cows and gold.
We had more wealth than we could use,
and many thus lived well.

94.   I paid a dowry for your hand
of treasures and of gems,
of thirty slaves and seven maids,
and silver most of all.

95.   You said you cared for nothing else
        if Buðli's lands lay fallow.
        You undermined my every word,
        so none received their shares.
        You always made my mother cry,
        my house was never home."

96.   "I do not care to hear your lies,
        if I am cruel, you're worse!
        You fought your brothers in your youth,
        and half you sent to hell!

97.   I felt invincible with mine
        and Sigurð by my side!
        We left the land, and sailed the sea
        until we reached the east.

98.   We slaughtered kings and seized their land,
        they bowed to us in fear.
        We rescued outlaws from the woods
        and made the peasants rich.

99.   When Sigurð died, I lost my will,
        too young was I a widow.
        To marry you was quite a loss
        compared to such a man!

100.   You've never come from any Thing
        with legal victories,
        you'd never hold your ground, but you'd
        surrender silently."

101.   "Now you're the one who's spreading lies,
        but this will do no good!
        Make sure I'm buried well, my wife,
        ensure our honor holds!"

102.   "I'll buy a ship and painted coffin
        and wrap your body well,
        and none will have a cause to think
        we felt a thing but love."

103.   Then Atli passed, aggrieved his kin,
        and Guðrun kept her word.
        She sought to bring about her death,
        but that would have to wait.

104.   Well-blessed is one whose children are
        as brave as Gjuki's brood,
        as long as people live to hear,
        their deeds will never die!

Guðrúnarhvøt

Guðrun's Fury

Introduction

Guðrúnarhvǫt "Guðrun's Incitement" is a short poem detailing how Guðrun drives her two youngest sons, Hamðir and Sorli, to avenge the murder of their elder sister Svanhild by her husband Jormunrekk and her final lament for all the troubles she faced in her life.

The story told in both this poem and *Hamðismál* also appears to be based on a real event. The 6th-century historian Jordanes, in his Latin history *De Origine Actibusque Getarum* tells of a 4th-century Gothic king named Ermanaric (whose name is a clear cognate of the Norse Jormunrekk), who ordered the drawing and quartering of a woman named Sunilda (Norse *Svanhildr*), whereupon her brothers Ammius (Norse *Hamðir*) and Sarius (Norse *Sørli*) attacked and injured Ermanaric. This almost exactly describes the plot of *Hamðismál*.

Guðrúnarhvǫt's beginning bears some similarities of phrasing to the beginning of *Hamðismál*, while its lament section is similar to the other Guðrun laments. Thus, the poem is likely a later work composed by someone familiar with these existing traditions.

After she killed Atli, Guðrun dove into the sea, hoping to end her life. She did not die, but was swept across the sea to the lands of King Jonak, and married him. They had three sons: Sorli, Erp, and Hamðir. Jonak also adopted Svanhild, Guðrun's daughter by Sigurð, and eventually married her off to Jormunrekk, the king of the Goths. Jormunrekk had an adviser named Bikki, who claimed Svanhild was having an affair with Randver, the king's son.[118] Jormunrekk then had Randver hanged, and Svanhild trampled to death by horses. When Guðrun heard of this, she gathered her sons and incited them to vengeance.

1. I heard a tale of woe and death,
    a grieving mother's wrath,
    when Guðrun stoked her sons' revenge
    with words both fierce and cruel.

2. "Why sit and sleep your lives away?
    Why speak of happy things
    when Jormunrekk's had Svanhild killed
    beneath a storm of hooves
    upon the Gothic battle-road
    by steeds both black and white?

3. You're not like Gunnar or his men,
    you're lacking Hogni's heart!
    If you had Niflung bravery,
    or hardy Hunnish souls,
    or spirit like my brothers had,
    you'd go avenge her death!"

4. Then Hamðir, bold of heart, declared:
    "You didn't praise your kin
    when they had Sigurð roused from sleep!
    The sheets you weaved him, blue and white,
    were reddened by his blood!

5. You got the worst revenge for them
    by slaughtering your sons!
    We would all slaughter Jormunrekk
    if we could fight as one!

---

[118] According to *Þiðreks Saga*, Bikki's motive for this was Jormunrekk's rape of his wife.

6.   But bring your Hunnish treasures here,
       we'll take revenge for you."

7.   She laughed, and gathered from her chests
       the helms and mail of kings
       and gifted them to both her sons
       as they prepared to go.

8.   Then Hamðir, bold of heart, declared:
       "May we return as Njorðs of spear[119]
       who fell in Gothic lands,
       when you would drink the mourning-ale
       for Svanhild and your sons!"

9.   Then Guðrun, Gjuki's daughter, wept
       and sat upon the porch.
       With rainy cheeks she told the tale
       of all that she'd endured.

10.   "I've lit three fires in three hearths,
       three husbands I have had,
       but Sigurð was the best of them,
       the man my brothers killed!

11.   There was no greater wound for me
       my brothers could inflict
       than making me be Atli's wife,
       I could not suffer more!

12.   I called my little cubs to me
       away from Atli's eyes.
       My troubles could not be resolved
       until their heads were gone!

13.   And then I sought the sea's embrace
       to curse the spiteful Norns.
       The stormy billows raised me up
       so live I reached the land.

____

[119] Kenning for *warriors*.

14.	Though death would be a better fate,
	I took another man.
	I bore three sons to Jonak's line,
	the heirs of all he has.

15.	And Svanhild's maids surrounded her,
	the best of all I've birthed.
	My daughter lived within my hall,
	as gorgeous as the sun!

16.	I sent her off with gold and silk
	to Jormunrekk's domain.
	I cannot bear her golden locks
	all matted in the mud.

17.	I grieved the most when Sigurð fell
	beside me in my bed,
	I cried the most when Gunnar's gut
	was split by shining snakes,
	It stung the most when Hogni's heart
	was cut from his brave chest.

18.	Too many evils have I known,
	now, Sigurð, mount your speedy horse
	as black as night, and run!
	There are no women in my house
	who'll share their wealth with me!

19.	Do you recall the words you said
	when we were in your bed?
	You said you'd come from hell to earth
	and I the other way!

20.	Now build a pyre out of oak,
	the best beneath the sky!
	May fire burn my grief away
	and melt my heavy heart!

21.	May every man find happiness,
	may women weep no more,
	may none know suffering again
	who've heard of all I've lost!"

Hamðismál

Hamðir's Vengeance

Introduction

Hamðismál "Hamðir's Words" is the final poem contained in the *Codex Regius*. It tells the other side of the story of *Guðrúnarhvǫt*; where that poem tells of Guðrun's reaction to her sons' departure, *Hamðismál* tells of Hamðir and Sorli's vengeance against Jormunrekk; they succeed in crippling the king at the cost of their lives, thus bringing the story of the Niflungs to a final, appropriately dramatic end.

As mentioned previously, this poem is based on real events that occurred in the 5th century. Its metrical structure is quite similar to that of *Atlakviða*, with much looser syllabic structure and patterning, which suggests that the poem is on the older side. The events of this poem are also alluded to in the 9th-century skaldic poem *Ragnarsdrápa*, though it is unlikely that poem's author had access to *Hamðismál* as we know it today. Stories of Hamðir and Sorli's revenge were probably told for centuries before the two of them were made sons of Guðrun and incorporated into the Niflung stories. It seems likely that *Hamðismál* is a 9th or 10th-century poem, based on material much older than that.

This is called *The Ancient Tale of Hamðir*.

1.   Upon the tree of fate once grew
the joyless grief of elves.
In early morning, evil deeds
were kindled for mankind!

2.   It wasn't now, or yesterday,
it happened long ago,
when Guðrun, Gjuki's daughter, roused
her sons to bloody wrath.

3.   "Your sister, Svanhild, lies a corpse,
run down by Jormunrekk
upon the Gothic army-road
by horses black and white.

4.   You're all the kin that I have left,
you should be flush with rage!

5.   I'm lonely as an aspen tree
or firs without their boughs.
My joy's been stripped like trees of leaves
upon a windy day!"

6.   Then Hamðir, brave of heart, declared:
"When Sigurð woke from sleep,
you had no praise for Hogni's deeds,
you slept, his killers laughed!

7.   The sheets you wove him, blue and white,
were reddened by his blood.
You sat by Sigurð's heatless corpse
without a joyous thought,
for Gunnar willed it so!

8.   You struck at Atli, killed his boys,
and how'd that go for you?
We all should wield a biting blade
in ways that spare ourselves."

9.   Then clever-minded Sorli said:
        "You've both no lack of words!
        I will not argue with my mom,
        although I'll ask her this:
        What fate do you foresee for us
        that will not cause you tears?

10.   You mourned your brothers and your sons,
        the kin you led to death.
        You'll weep for both of us as well,
        we're doomed upon our steeds
        to die in distant lands!"

11.   They then departed Jonak's lands,
        their roars made mountains shake!
        They went across the rainy peaks
        with vengeance on their minds.

12.   They met a man along the road
        whose strategies were sharp.
        "How can a dwarf with ruddy hair
        be any use to us?"

13.   Their father's son said he could help
        like feet help other feet.
        "How can a foot help other feet,
        or hands help other hands?"

14.   Then Erp responded famously
        from on his horse's back:
        "It's bad to show the weak the way!"
        "You're brave, as bastards go!"

15.   From scabbards came their shining blades,
        to devils' great delight.
        They cut their number by a third,
        and put him in the dirt.

16.   They shook their cloaks and sheathed their swords,
        and dressed in fancy clothes.

17.	They found young Randver on a rope
	upon a tree of wolves.[120]
	They'd speared him west of where the hall
	of Jormunrekk was built.
	His dangling body baited birds,
	'twas not a happy sight!

18.	The Gothic halls were full of cheer
	and men stuffed full of ale.
	They did not hear the boys approach
	until they blew their horn.

19.	The guards then told king Jormunrekk
	that armored men had come:
	"Be careful, mighty men are here!
	Your murder drew their rage!"

20.	He laughed and stroked his ruddy beard,
	his wine igniting rage.
	He raised his pearly shield aloft
	and twirled his golden cup.

21.	"If Gjuki's boys have traveled here,
	then I'm a blessed man!
	I'll use their bows to string them up
	and hang them by my son!"

22.	Beside the doors stood Hroðrgloð,
	who told the youthful king:
	"They promise many valiant deeds
	they have no hope to do!
	Can two men beat two hundred Goths
	within their mighty fort?"

23.	Then battle came, and scattered cups
	as well as Gothic blood.

---

[120] A gallows.

24.   Then Hamðir, brave of heart, declared:
"You hoped we'd travel here,
so you could see us killed!
But now you see your hands and feet
as ashes in your hearth!"

25.   The king of godly blood called out,
his roar surpassed a bear's:
"The sons of Jonak can't be harmed
by iron; stone them down!"

26.   Then clever-minded Sorli said:
"You've badly erred this time
by loosening that bag,[121]
for bags can still give orders, fool!

27.   You lack the brains to have a mind,
for fools are missing much!

28.   He'd have no head if Erp were here,
our brother, who we killed!
The disir urged us both to end
that valiant warrior!"

29.   Then Hamðir, brave of heart, declared:
"We shouldn't fight like wolves,
the greedy bitches of the Norns,
who spill their kinsmen's blood
and gorge themselves in wildlands!

30.   We stand on hills of Gothic dead
like eagles on a branch!
We've slaughtered well, and earned our fame
no matter when we die,
for no one lives a single night
beyond the Norns' decree!"

31.   Then Sorli fell before the doors,
and Hamðir at the back.

---

[121] i.e, by giving Jormunrekk a chance to talk. The "bag" is his mangled torso.

Glossary: The Names of the Edda

Aegir: "sea".

Afi: "grandfather".

Agnar: "sword-edge warrior".

Ai: "great-grandfather".

Alf: "elf".

Alfoðr: "All-Father".

Alsvið: "Very Fast".

Alviss: "All-Wise".

Alvit: Either "all-wise" or "foreigner"

Alþjolf: "All-Thief".

Amma: "grandmother".

An: probably a contraction of *aðal vinr*, "noble friend".

Annar: "second".

Andvari: "the anxious one".

Angantyr: "smelly god".

Arvak: "early riser".

Asgarð: "domain of the gods".

Atli: "cruel one".

Atrið: "battle-rider".

Aurgelmir: "mud-roarer".

Aurvang: "mud field".

Baldr: "brave one" or "prince".

Baleyg: "blaze-eye".

Bavor: unclear, possibly a meaningless phonetic alteration of *Bivor*.

Bergelmir: "mountain yeller".

Beyla: unclear, possibly related to *baun* "bean".

Biflindi: "shield-shaker".

Bikki: probably "bitch".

Bild: "blade".

Bileyg: "gap eye" (in reference to Oðin's missing eye).

Billing: "twin".

Bilskirnir: "shining moment". The name possibly refers to flashing lightning.

Bivor: "shaker".

Bolverker: "evildoer".

Bombur: either "drummer" or "fat one".

Bor: "drill".

Borghild: "battle-protection".

Boðvild: "kind offer".

Bragi: "noble one" or "poet".

Breiðablik: "broad glimmer".

Bruni: "brown one".

Brynhild: "armored warrior".

Buri: either "resident" or "son".

Buðli: "offerer".

Byggvir: "barley man".

Dain: "one that has died".

Delling: "bright one".

Dolgþrasir: "vicious enemy".

Draupnir: "dripper".

Durin: either "sleepy" or "door".

Dvalin: "slowpoke".

Edda: "great-grandmother". This name is not related to the title of this book.

Eggþer: "sword-bearer".

Egil: "terrifier".

Eikinskjaldi: "oaken shield".

Eikþyrnir: "oak-thorn".

Eldir: "fire-maker".

Fafnir: "embracer".

Falhofnir: "hidden-hoofed".

Farmatyr: "Cargo-God".

Faðir: "father".

Fenja: "(woman) of the swamps".

374

Fenrir: probably "swamp-dweller".

Fensalir: "swamp hall".

Fili: either "file" or "board".

Fimafeng: "fast gain".

Fimbultyr: "mighty god".

Fimbulvetr: "mighty winter".

Finn: "Sami" (a Finnic people indigenous to Northern Europe).

Fjalar: "hider".

Fjolnir: possibly "multiplier".

Fjolsvið: "very wise".

Fjorgyn: from an old Germanic root meaning "mountain".

Folkvang: "army-field".

Fornbogi: "old bow".

Fraeg: "famous one".

Frar: "fast".

Freki: "ravenous one".

Frey: "lord".

Freyja: "lady".

Frigg: "beloved".

Frosti: "frost".

Froði: "wise one".

Fundin: "found one".

Gagnrað: "useful advisor".

Gandalf: "staff-elf".

Gangleri: "wanderer".

Garm: Unknown. Possibilites include "growler" and "ragged one".

Gaut: "person", a poetic term from *gautr* "Goth".

Geirolul: the first element is *geirr* "spear", but the second is uncertain.

Geirroð: "spear-reddener".

Geirskogul: "spear-shaker".

Geri: "greedy one".

Gerð: "enclosed one".

Ginnar: "liar".

Gisl: "hostage".

Gjuki: possibly "giver".

Glaer: "clear one".

Glapsvið: "trick master".

Glað: either "bright one" or "happy one".

Glaðsheim: either "bright home" or "happy home".

Glitnir: "glitterer".

Gloin: "glowing one".

Goll: "shriek".

Gondlir: "staff-wielder".

Gondul: "staff-user".

Grani: either "spruce" or "mustachioed one".

Grim: "mask".

Grimhild: "masked battle".

Grimnir: "masked one".

Gripir: probably "gripper".

Gulltopp: "gold locks".

Gullinkamb: "golden comb".

Gullrond: "gold strand".

Gullveig: either "gold power", or "gold booze".

Gunnar: "war-army".

Gutthorm: "divine respect".

Guðmund: "divine protection".

Guðrun: "secret of battle".

Gyllir: "gold one".

Hagall: "hail".

Hamðir: "servant of flesh".

Hannar: "skilled one".

Har: "high one".

Harbarð: "grey beard".

Hati: "hater".

Haugspori: "barrow-spur".

Heimdall: "world-lighter".

Heið: "bright one".

Heiðrun: "bright secret".

Helblindi: "hell-blind".

Helgi: "holy one".

Hepti: "haft"

Herfjotur: "army-chain".

Herjafoðr: "army father".

Herjan: "army leader".

Herteit: "army-glad".

Hervor: "army-aware".

Heðin: "hooded one".

Hild: "battle".

Himinbjorg: "sky mountain".

Hjalmberi: "helmet-bearer".

Hjordis: "sword lady".

Hjorvarð: "sword-guardian".

Hlevang: "shelter field".

Hlokk: either "scream" or "clatter".

Hlorriði: "loud rider".

Hloð: probably "slaughterer".

Hnikar: "inciter".

Hnikuð: same as above.
378

Hogni: "skilled one".

Honir: Unclear. Possibly related to *høna* "hen" or an old Germanic root meaning "white one".

Hoð: "fight".

Hoðbrodd: "spike-battle".

Hraesvelg: "wreck-swallower".

Hrimfaxi: "frost mane".

Hrimgerð: "frostbound".

Hropt: "sage".

Hroðmar: "praise-horse".

Hrungnir: "fighter".

Hrym: probably "wimp", from *hrumr* "frail".

Hugin: "thought".

Humli: "hops" (the plant).

Hunding: "hound-born".

Hymir: uncertain, possibly "weary one" or "cheapskate".

Hyndla: "little bitch".

Iðavell: either "plain of activity" or "plain of whirlpools".

Iðun: "active one".

Jafnhar: "equal-high".

Jalk: "gelding".

Jari: "conflict".

Jonak: uncertain. Possibly from a Slavic root meaning "young man".

Jormungand: "big snake" or "big monster".

Jormunrekk: "grand champion".

Kili: "keel".

Kjallar: "keeler".

Knefroð: "knee-wise".

Kon: a shortening of *konungr*, "king".

Lettfeti: "light foot".

Lit:- "color".

Loki: probably "tangler", from an old Germanic word for "loop".

Loni: "calm water".

Loður: either "hairy one" or "fruitful one".

Magni: "power".

Menja: "(woman) of the necklaces".

Mimir: perhaps "the mindful one"

Miðgarð: "middle enclosure".

Mjolnir: "grinder".

Mjoðvitnir: "mead monster".

Mogþrasir: "stubborn kinsman".

Moði: "fury".

Moðir: "mother".

Moðsognir: "furious sucker".
380

Mundilfari: "timed traveler".

Munin: "memory".

Nain: either "close one" or "corpse-ish one".

Nali: "nail".

Nar: "corpse".

Niflhel: "mist-hell".

Niflung: "mistborn".

Niping: possibly "drooper".

Niðavoll: "dark plain".

Niðhogg: "dishonorable attacker".

Niði: "new moon".

Niðuð: "dishonorable character".

Njorð: uncertain. Possibly related to Old Irish *nert* "power".

Noatun: "enclosure of ships".

Nori: "little guy".

Norr: "narrow one".

Ny: "new".

Nyi: "full moon".

Nyrað: "new advice".

Oddrun: "secret of spear-points".

Oin: "timid one".

Olrun: "beer-secret".

Omi: "noisy one".

Ottar: "feared army".

Oski: "wished-for".

Oskopnir: "not made".

Oð: "fury", "ecstasy", and/or "inspiration".

Oðin: "furious/ecstatic/inspired one".

Oðrerir: "spirit-stirrer".

Ran: "robber".

Randgrið: "shield-greed".

Randver: "shield man".

Ratatosk: "drill-tusk".

Raðgrið: "peaceful advice".

Raðsvið: "wise advice", from *ráð* + *svið*,

Regin: "commander".

Reginleif: "divine relic".

Rig: "king", a loan from Old Irish *rí*.

Saga: unclear, maybe "prophet".

Sanngetall: "truth-getter".

Sað: "truthful".

Sigfoðr: "father of victory".

Sigmund: "victory-protector".

Sigrdrifa: "victory-driver".

Sigrlin: "victory-snake".

Sigrun: "victory-secret".

Sigurð: probably a contraction of *Sigvarð*, "victory guardian".

Silfrintopp: "silver locks".

Sinfjotli: uncertain, possibly "sparkle-foot".

Sinir: "muscular one".

Siðgrani: "wide mustache".

Siðhott: "wide hat".

Siðskegg: "broad beard".

Skafið: "careful Sami".

Skaði: either "harm" or "shadow".

Skeiðbrimir: "surging racer".

Skeggjold: "era of axes".

Skilfing: "prince".

Skinfaxi: "bright mane".

Skirnir: "shining one".

Skiðblaðnir: "made of wood chips".

Skogul: "trembler".

Skoll: either "traitor" or "mocker".

Skuld: "obligation", from *skuld* "debt".

Slagfið: "striking Sami".

Sokkvabekk: "sunken bank".

Sorli: either "defender" or "clever one".

Svafnir: "sleep bringer".

Svalin: "cold one".

Svanhild: "swan-battle".

Svanhvit: "swan-white".

Svasuð: "delightful".

Svava: "Swabian".

Svipall: "shifter".

Sviur: "Swede".

Svið: "wise one".

Sviðrir: either "burner" or "calm-bringer".

Sviður: "wise one".

Tyr: "god".

Tyrfing: "(blade) of the Visigoths".

Ull: "glorious one".

Urð: "fate".

Uð: "wave".

Vafþruðnir: "great weaver".

Vak: "waker".

Vaðgelmir: "wade-screamer".

Valaskjalf: "slaughter-shelf".

Valfoðr: "Slaughter-Father".

Valhall: "slaughter hall".

Vali: "little warrior".

Valtam: "slaughter-accustomed".

Var: "vow".

Vegtam: "road-accustomed".

Veig: either "booze" or "power".

Verðandi: "happening", present participle of *verða* "to become".

Vigrið: "battle-ride".

Vili: "struggler".

Vindalf: "wind elf".

Vindsval: "wind-cold".

Vingi: contraction of *vin eigi*, "not a friend".

Vit: "wise one".

Viðar: "wide army".

Viði: "woods".

Viðrir: "stormer".

Viður: "slayer".

Volund: from a Germanic root meaning "craftsman". Written *Wayland* in this book to fit with this character's Old English name.

Ygg: "terrifying".

Yggdrasil: "Ygg's horse". A likely reference to Oðin's having hanged himself on this tree. Kennings for *gallows* often invoke horses.

Ylfing: "wolf-born".

Ymir: either "groaner" or from an old root meaning "twin".

Þekk: "agreeable one".

Þjoðrek: "great king".

Þor: "thunder". Not the usual word for *thunder* in Old Norse (which is *þurma)*, but definitely related to English *thunder*, German *Donar*, etc.

Þorin: "brave one".

Þrain: either "stubborn one" or "pining one".

Þror: "flourishing one".

Þriði: "third".

Þruðgelmir: "powerful yeller".

Þruðheim: "strong home".

Þrym: "clamor".

Þrymheim: "noisy home".

Þund: uncertain, perhaps "booming one" or "extended one".

Hoc opus est scrīptum; egeō pōtū. Deus adiūtet manūs meī.

The work is finished; I need a drink. May God help my hands.